THE MODERN MIXOLOGIST

Tony Abou-Ganim with Mary Elizabeth Faulkner

THE MODERN MIXOLOGIST

CONTEMPORARY CLASSIC COCKATILS

SURREY BOOKS

AN AGATE IMPRINT

CHICAGO

Book design and layout: Brandtner Design

Printed in China.

Library of Congress Cataloging-in-Publication Data

Abou-Ganim, Tony.
    The modern mixologist : contemporary classic cocktails / Tony Abou-Ganim with Mary Elizabeth Faulkner.
        p. cm.
    Includes bibliographical references and index.
    Summary: "A cocktail guide for the 21st century, complete with 60 recipes for new and classic drinks.
Full-color photography throughout, with tips on ingredients, barware, and technique"--Provided by publisher.
    ISBN-13: 978-1-57284-107-9 (hardcover)
    ISBN-10: 1-57284-107-9 (hardcover)
1. Cocktails. I. Faulkner, Mary Elizabeth. II. Title.
    TX951.A295 2010
    641.8'74--dc22
                        2009046340

10 9 8 7 6 5 4 3 2 1

Surrey Books is an imprint of Agate Publishing. Agate books are available in bulk at discount prices.
For more information, go to agatepublishing.com.

To the memory of Helen and Neva, two impressively strong women. Both had a wonderful respect for the bartender's craft and great appreciation for a well-made drink. Happiness!

Table of Contents

Mario Batali and Tony Abou-Ganim, October 7, 2009.

Foreword

IN MY SHORT LIFE, the sophistication of the American diner has swung like a pendulum from the vast extremes of the banal, such as pure comfort food, to the pioneer, such as molecular gastronomy. Since the invention of the light bulb in Menlo Park in the late 1870s, life has changed much for seekers of "restoration" in a restaurant, tavern, or bar. Our methods and needs of consuming calories as fuel for our bodies has changed just as much. The alchemy of preparing the restorative libation has changed radically as well in both conceptualization and execution. Cooks and barkeeps, once on the lower end of the social strata, have achieved rock star status for their ability to transform what was merely energy replacement into something entirely new and exciting for the modern generation of restoration-seekers.

This brings me to Tony Abou-Ganim—rock star, bar chef, cocktail wizard, restoration specialist. When we first met, Tony was a cappuccino expert who opened wine bottles for a busy little trattoria in the West Village. What struck me most was his unwavering understanding of the nature of hospitality. The warm welcome, the extension of self, and the maniacal attention to every guest's needs and whims for the achievement of their comfort was his mantra and his gift. And he still has it.

What a surprise...

Fast forward fifteen years and Tony has passed through the Dale DeGroff-guarded gates of cocktail Zen mastery, developed and departed the cocktail program at the mythic Bellagio Hotel in Las Vegas, and is now well established in his position as grand master of the new world of cocktails as a way of life. I now see Tony headline events at the Food and Wine Classic in Aspen, the South Beach Food and Wine Festival, New York, Big Island, Newport Beach... . Anywhere they wanted chefs ten years ago, they now want mixologists, too, and Tony Abou-Ganim is the poster boy for modern mixology.

As in the world of food, the poetry of local, seasonal, fresh ingredients and the idiom of the traditional versus the modern and creative, kind of drive the PR boat. Tony and I agree on just about all of these things. We love tradition more than the merely new; we love the seasonal change of climate and its affect on the thirsts and hungers of our constituency; and above all, we love the feeling we get when we can extend ultimate hospitality to someone who understands and appreciates it. As with the new world of food and wine in restaurants, the new world of cocktail wizardry is merely an extension of the most basic and classic form of hospitality. The new generation is the conduit, and Tony Abou-Ganim is the beverage guy. So read this book and treat your friends or guests to the best you can offer them.

MARIO BATALI

Introduction to Mixology

"What are we having next?"... To my simple mind this is an awesome phrase. It's filled with positive expectation, change, variety, sociability and unity. And in my world probably leads to a drink...

ANGUS WINCHESTER, INDUSTRY EXPERT

I BECAME HOOKED ON BARTENDING on my birthday in 1978, while seated at the bar of the Brass Rail, my cousin Helen's place in Port Huron, Michigan. I was celebrating my very first evening of legal drinking with my parents. Up to this point, I had spent many family occasions in this bar with its fascinating array of bottles and bartending gadgets, shiny mirrors, polished brass, and warm, perennially friendly atmosphere.

Growing up, I watched in awe as my uncles Sol, Charlie, and Tony worked smoothly behind the great bar in their starched white shirts. Up to this point, this had always been their world to which I'd been a welcome visitor who might be treated to a Roy Rogers or two. This night was different. I marveled at the endless stream of cocktails being lined up in my honor, all of them, I would come to learn, true classics. Something clicked that evening and little did I know that I had been captured by this world—hook, line, and sinker.

Eventually I went to work behind the bar at the Brass Rail, where I mixed my first cocktail in the fall of 1980. I don't remember which one exactly, but let's just say it wouldn't have won any awards. My apprenticeship was relatively informal, but rigorous nonetheless. Under the watchful eye of Helen and the rest of my bar-savvy family, I quickly discovered an art to tending bar far beyond anything I had previously considered. True, it wasn't the Ritz or Waldorf-Astoria, but I discovered a great integrity and passion in my mentors' professional demeanor and dedication to serving customers. There was never a question of forsaking quality in the pursuit of profits. Cocktails were made according to their original recipes and methods, and always with high-quality ingredients. I soon realized that I couldn't fake a good drink and I wouldn't win any customers trying. As Helen used to say, "For a nickel more you go first class!"—a sentiment that stays with me to this day.

Bartending, like so many professions, has a wonderful camaraderie among its ranks, and fortunately for me it's a skill that travels extremely well. Like many, I initially used bartending to see me through college and pay the rent while I pursued other interests—primarily acting. Eventually, and in some ways without realizing it, I became irrevocably dedicated to the profession.

I have always been most at home when behind the bar, doing my part to see the weight of the world lifted from my customers' shoulders, even if only for a short time. I will never tire of seeing someone truly excited about a really well-crafted cocktail, regardless of whether it is one of mine or one of the classics. I find it both unique and energizing to be able to engineer that experience for another person, and even more amazing to watch as they share it with someone else—sharing the love, so to speak. I suppose what really fuels my passion for this profession is that power to spread cheer. Fortunately, I've made it to a place in my professional life where I now have the opportunity to share my enthusiasm for premium cocktails with the world. I realize bartending is neither rocket science nor brain surgery, and it is never going to cure the ills of this world. But while enjoying drinks outside one balmy evening in Las Vegas—the Lake Bellagio water show as our backdrop—my dear friend and writing partner pointed out that "spreading the love" through cocktails is still a gift of some significance to those seeking a little escape from life's day-to-day rigors.

THE RESURGENCE OF THE COCKTAIL

WE ARE FULLY IN THE MIDST of a cocktail and spirits renaissance. Aside from a renewed interest in classic cocktails, the past twenty years have seen a marked new appreciation for the barman's craft, and a growing interest in applying culinary creativity toward producing ingenious new cocktails.

Romance aside, however, the majority of bar professionals must still operate within the ebb and flow of what is a monstrously powerful industry. In short, spirits and their companion cocktails can be made hugely popular through the sheer power of money and marketing. However, overwhelming popularity does not necessarily equate to a premium product.

Though money and marketing have long determined the popularity of certain drinks, the concept of drinking "better" rather than "more" has finally seeped into the collective cocktail consciousness. While many working behind the stick may be limited by less-than-premium materials, selected by employers of varying motivations, the rest of us interested in creating delicious drinks at home finally have the spirits, the resources, and the experts needed for help in this pursuit. There is no longer any reason to partake of a substandard cocktail. And there is no reason you shouldn't be able to recognize quality when it is being served—or specify quality when it may be lacking.

The finer points of the culinary arts for the home chef have long been promoted and embraced, by voices ranging from Julia Child to Alice Waters and Jacques Pépin to Thomas Keller and Mario Batali and so many others. An amazing meal paired with a fine wine is an experience nearly everyone can appreciate. Naturally, as one whose world essentially revolves around spirits and the enjoyment thereof, I believe that creating an exquisite mixed drink recipe—or more to the point, promoting the beauty of drinks built with an epicurean tilt— is a fledgling arm of the same culinary movement. Whatever the cuisine, there is a drink recipe to enhance the experience. The door is now open wide, and it's time to cross the threshold to explore the possibilities.

MIXOLOGIST OR "BARTENDER?"

What exactly makes a mixologist? For me, it lies in the ability to meld the classic and the contemporary, infusing the art of classic cocktail making with modern culinary ingredients and ingenuity—hence the latest industry moniker, "bar chef."

I approach crafting an original libation much as a chef would approach creating a new entrée, seeking the best combination of ingredients to please the palate. You have to recognize the flavor profile of each ingredient and how they interact to influence and compliment each other. This is the big secret to excelling in mixology—and this is where diligent work pays off—tasting, tasting, and more tasting. You have to *try* things to understand how they taste, and, more importantly, how they perform in a drink among other ingredients.

A good friend, Steve Olson of "AKA Wine Geek" fame, taught me a long time ago to keep an imaginary book in my mind, in which to make "notes" every time I tasted something so I could remember its unique characteristics. Over the years this simple exercise has helped me build up a vast library of flavors to use in conjuring new cocktail recipes. Don't be afraid to consider your flavor preferences in all areas—not only spirits and liqueurs, but also mixers, fresh fruits, juices, purées, herbs, florals, and even vegetables.

THE FIRST STEP

So where to start? Mark Twain once said, "Part of the secret of success in life is to eat what you like." I would venture to guess he would have included "drink what you like" as well. Too often, I see people basing their drinking decisions on what is hip at the moment. The fact is, what sells the most in terms of volume is generally media-driven (and therefore industry-driven), the product of whatever a particular spirit company's immense marketing budget is pushing. This does not, of course, necessarily make it the best choice for you. There are a significant number of smaller producers making outstanding spirits, and there is great fun to be had in the hunt.

When it comes to learning your own drink preferences, you need to start somewhere. Why not begin at your favorite bar? It can be intimidating to venture into the unknown. I see it all the time. Someone stands at the bar, clearly a bit unsettled by the scene—perhaps even by the bartender, who might appear a little aloof to the novice. The patron seems unsure of what or maybe even how to order something new. Nervous, the customer usually just says, "gin and tonic," or "rum and coke," or the easiest of all, "I'll have a beer."

Do not fear. A good bartender will take the time to inquire about your preferences and make appropriate suggestions. Before long you'll have a much better sense of why you like what you like. Now you are armed and ready to venture into the art of mixology.

ART OVER SCIENCE

> *Cooking is a creation…. It is how we share our sense of art, our knowledge, and our taste with other people.* **Piero Selvaggio**

When setting out to create a great cocktail, there are a few key concepts to keep in mind:

1. **Less is more.** Consider the majority of classics cocktails that have survived the test of

time. Many are relatively simple concoctions. The quintessential cocktail, for example, the classic Martini, consists of just two ingredients. It is the choice of these ingredients, the style and quality of the gin and vermouth, and how they are handled—rather, married together—that makes a great Martini great. The Manhattan, made of straight rye whiskey, Italian sweet vermouth, and Angostura bitters, is simple yet sultry. The Daiquiri is a classic that, in its original form, is also elegantly simple, composed of light-bodied rum, fresh-squeezed lime juice, and sugar.

2. **Take a straightforward and logical approach.** Anyone can make great cocktails themselves, so why is it that so few people actually do? We are no longer recovering from Prohibition, when the booze was so awful that people had to disguise it with a myriad of syrups and mixers just to choke it down. Honestly, there is no deep, dark secret to preparing wonderful cocktails, exclusive to those of us who have spent our lives pursuing it. Avoid a haphazard approach to mixing drinks. Throwing a miscellaneous selection of spirits, liqueurs, cordials, syrups, juices, cream, eggs, fruits, and artificial mixers into a shaker with ice does not a cocktail make. Consider the base spirit and how it is best complemented; think about your accents and modifiers; and keep it simple.

3. **Every cocktail recipe starts with a base spirit.** Understanding a cocktail's structure is crucial. Each is essentially defined through its base spirit, be it gin, vodka, tequila, rum, brandy, or whiskey. This spirit should make up the majority of your cocktail. Consider a culinary comparison: you don't prepare a rib-eye steak for the salt and pepper, so stay away from drowning your spirit in accoutrements. The Margarita, for example, should always be about the tequila; the Cointreau and fresh lime juice work to enhance the tequila's unique nuances, not to cover them up. The Margarita is, and should always be, a tequila drink—replace the spirit and it becomes something else altogether.

4. **Explore modifiers and accents.** Here is the spice of the drink-making world. Modifiers are made up of various aromatic wines—for example, vermouth and Lillet—and a long list of liqueurs, such as Cointreau, maraschino, and crème de cassis. Accents include different varieties of bitters—like orange, Peychaud's, and Angostura—and non-alcoholic syrups—including Rose's lime juice, orgeat, grenadine, and falernum. In the Manhattan, for example, the base spirit is rye whiskey, the modifier is Italian sweet vermouth, and the accent is Angostura bitters. One of the things that's especially fun about mixology is that

modifiers and accents can be used interchangeably; that is, in some cases the line between the two is blurred. Fresh fruit juices (lemon, lime, orange, grapefruit, pineapple), sugars (simple syrup, gum [gomme] syrup, rock candy, honey, agave nectar), cream, and even eggs can serve as either a modifier or an accent. The options are vast, so prepare to flex those adventurous tendencies when exploring the world of modifiers and accents. Just remember their subordinate place within the mixology palate.

5. **Balance above all else.** Strive for balance in your cocktail. To make another culinary comparison—if you put too much garlic in the gravy, what stands out? Consider the same dynamic in a cocktail—too much lemon juice in a Collins and your mouth will instantly pucker in protest. Your drink should strike a balance between the flavors of alcohol, sweet, acid, tart, and bitter. Achieving balance gets easier with practice—lots of practice—but you'll never learn to find the point of equilibrium unless you take the time to taste as you go.

6. **Never skimp on quality.** As mentioned, most classic cocktails consist of at most three or maybe four ingredients. The quality of those ingredients ultimately dictate the outcome of your drink. You can't build a Ferrari out of Ford parts. If you want an exceptional cocktail, always, I repeat, always use quality ingredients.

BRINGING IT HOME

I'LL NEVER TIRE OF CRAFTING the perfect cocktail or cocktail experience. Within these pages there is neither an encyclopedia of drink recipes nor a discourse about professional bartending. Instead you will find a celebration of the cocktail experience—the art of creating and enjoying amazing cocktails.

You will notice I do not shy away from listing the names of specific products used in constructing these recipes. As you can imagine, the selection of a particular spirit when creating a cocktail is entirely subjective, and in the case of this book reflects my personal taste. Since I hope you will try these recipes at home, I would feel remiss if I were not as specific as possible about what goes into them. Of course, these spirit selections were made to suit each individual drink recipe. However, there are so many other outstanding spirits, and so many creative possibilities and wonderful variations yet to be created, I encourage you experiment as freely as you wish!

May the inspiration for your next favorite cocktail be found within.

The Evolution of Mixology

History is based on fact, fiction, supposition, and a good imagination, especially if it benefits the individual writing it. All the so called historical elements that are referred to as valid, are only observations, impressions, oral statements, and the writers goal in placing his/her words in print, especially true during the period of the late 1800s and early 1900s.

Brian Rea

For me, the genesis of different drinks is a subject I never tire of exploring. When did consuming spirits become an iconic part of our culture? How did the simple act of throwing back a "drink" become enjoying a "cocktail?" Naturally there are no easy answers, with rather more gray areas than not. Yet between points A and B there are numerous historical events, inventions, and just plain accidents that all contributed to the evolution of cocktail culture and, ultimately, what I have come to appreciate and refer to as "modern mixology."

Having sifted through a variety of accounts, this is a mere nod toward what I consider to be the key eras, events, developments, and inventions along the mixology timeline—a look at the major milestones within the world of spirits, drinks culture, cocktails, and tending bar.

My rendition will no doubt face healthy criticism from industry gurus. Again, this is not a book about history, per se, but it's important to take a brief look at how history has influenced the way we enjoy cocktails today.

GOTHIC AGE: 1775-1830s

In the Gothic Age of American drinking and word making, between the Revolution and the Civil War, many fantastic drinks were invented, and given equally fantastic names: stone fence, blue blazer, and stinkibus...The touring Englishmen of those days always spread news of such grotesque drink names, some of these Columbuses embellished the list with outlandish inventions of their own...

H.L. MENCKEN, *THE AMERICAN LANGUAGE*

William Grimes, in his book *Straight Up or On The Rocks*, declares that the New World first experienced commercially distilled grain thanks to Wilhelm Kieft, director-general of what was then called New Netherland, who in 1640 erected a still for making gin. But I believe that the earliest significant development toward the practice of mixing drinks coincided roughly with the Revolutionary War: the creation of vermouth.

1786: Antonio Benedetto Carpano is the first to produce commercial vermouth in Turin, Italy. His was a "rosso," or sweet vermouth, which became known as the Italian style. By the turn of the century, in Marseillan, France, Joseph Noilly introduced a white wine-based "dry" vermouth. The earliest mixed drink recipes calling for vermouth, such as the **Martinez**, would have utilized the Italian-style vermouth. For the next century, vermouth was categorized as either Italian (sweet) or French (dry). Today, each country produces both varieties, and both are used in a wide variety of cocktails.

1780 TO 1827: Somewhere during this timeframe, the **Tom Collins** is created by a waiter at Limmer's Hotel on Conduit Street in London. His drink featured Old Tom, a sweetened gin. It wasn't until much later that the recipe found its way to the United States, at a time when dry gin had become the norm. Hence the difference between the Tom Collins and the **John Collins**—the former being made of Old Tom gin and the latter of Holland dry gin, respectively.

1820s: Pierce Egan is credited with popularizing one of my favorite cold weather warmers, the **Tom & Jerry**, an invention purported to be a marketing tool used to promote his book *Life in London, or The Day and Night Scenes of Jerry Hawthorn Esq. and his Elegant Friend Corinthian Tom* (1821).

1826: Scotsman Robert Stein patents the continuous still. Previously, distillation had been accomplished solely in pot stills, considerably less efficient than the newer, continuous method.

1830: Irishman Aeneas Coffey develops his eponymous Coffey still (also known as the "patent still"), leading ultimately to the development of blended Scotch whisky. The Coffey still could produce neutral grain spirit on a much larger scale than earlier stills.

EARLY NINETEENTH CENTURY: Commercial ice harvesting begins in the 1830s, allowing ice to be used more affordably by more barmen.

GOLDEN AGE: 1840s–1919

In Nevada, for a time, the lawyer, the editor, the banker, the chief desperado,
the chief gambler, and the saloon-keeper occupied the same level in society,
and it was the highest.

MARK TWAIN, *ROUGHING IT*

Pinning down the exact margins of the Golden Age of cocktails is difficult. Gary Regan, in his book *The Joy of Mixology*, believes it was during the 1890s, whereas Paul Harrington in his book, *Cocktail*, considers the 1860s more likely, while industry expert Brian Rea asserts that it began in the 1840s.

Without question, this Golden Age contributed more toward refining the craft and culture of classic cocktails than any period before or since. Many a classic cocktail was created. Mixologists became far more professional, and several began publishing their recipes. Some of the most gorgeous bars ever to exist were erected during this time—primarily in cities like New York, New Orleans, San Francisco, London, and Paris. It's impossible to hit all the highlights, but here are a few…

1856: According to the historian and author of *Imbibe!*, David Wondrich, the term "mixologist" first appears in print in a story published by Charles G. Leland in an issue of *Knickerbocker*, a New York literary journal. Wondrich explained to me that, with "…no word for a bartender who has unusual interest and expertise in mixing drinks, people [started] using 'Mixologist'.…The *Washington Post* later acknowledged this when it said, 'when [bartenders] become especially proficient at putting odds and ends of firewater together, they become Mixologists.'"

1859: The **Sazerac** is invented—purportedly the first cocktail of American origin, notable for its use of absinthe. This was originally a cognac-based drink, but eventually transitioned to an American-made whiskey base—rye, in fact, a more widely available alternative.

1862: Professor Jerry Thomas publishes the first-ever cocktail book, one of our profession's most highly coveted texts, *The Bar-tender's Guide*. I consider myself extremely fortunate to have an 1887 edition. Among so many other things, we learn that by this time ice is commonly used in drink preparation.

1864: The Hoffman House opens its doors. Considered one of New York's most elegant bars, it was home to veteran barman William F. Mulhall—who, according to William Grimes's *Straight Up or On The Rocks*, "claimed that the celebrated **Manhattan** Cocktail … was invented by a man named Black who kept a saloon on Broadway just below Houston Street. This runs counter to the more popular theory that the drink was created at the Manhattan Club in 1874, at a banquet to celebrate Governor Tilden's election victory."

1867: At some point following the Merchant Shipping Act of this year, which required all British merchant ships to provide lime juice to their crew in order to combat scurvy, Lauchlin Rose received a patent for preserving lime juice. Soon thereafter, Rose's Lime Juice was broadly available throughout the British Empire. It was some years later, perhaps after he joined the navy in 1879, that Sir Thomas D. Gimlette was credited with first mixing gin with Rose's Lime Juice, creating what is now popularly known as a **Gimlet**.

1870: According to Barnaby Conrad III in his book, *The Martini*, it is at Julio Richelieu's saloon in Martinez, California, where a small drink is mixed for a traveling miner...and it's called the **Martinez.** Is this, as many claim, the **Martini**'s predecessor? Martinez, California, continues to claim itself the Martini's birthplace. The city's memorial plaque to that effect even documents Richelieu's "Martinez Special" recipe—two-thirds gin, one-third vermouth, and a dash of orange bitters poured over crushed ice and finished with an olive. I like this story, because the proportions Richelieu used are close to what we know today as a Martini.

1882: Harry Johnson publishes his famous cocktail guide, *The Bartenders' Manual*. If there is anyone who can go toe to toe with Jerry Thomas as the Grandfather of Bartending, it would be Johnson. His wonderful book, written twenty years after Thomas's, is perhaps even rarer and more valuable, and is still a great source of information and insight into our craft.

1887: Jerry Thomas lays claim to creating the **Martinez** (or at the very least, his version of it), publishing the recipe in the 1887 edition of *The Bar-Tender's Guide*. The recipe called for a dash of Boker's bitters, 2 dashes of Maraschino liqueur, a pony of Old Tom gin, and a wine-glass (4 ounces) of vermouth (which would have meant sweet vermouth), along with the suggestion that, "If the guest prefers it very sweet, add two dashes of gum syrup." One can see that this is a far cry from what we know today as the Martini. It is, in fact, a Martinez and should be enjoyed as such, but do yourself a favor and leave out the gum syrup.

1888: At the Imperial Cabinet Saloon in New Orleans, Henry Ramos invents the **Ramos Gin Fizz**, a drink worthy of rediscovery and celebration. Also this year, Harry Johnson publishes the revised edition of his *New and Improved Illustrated Bartender's Manual or How To Mix Drinks of the Present Style*. Here the word "Martini" first appears.

1895: Patrick Gavin Duffy, who tended bar at the Ashland House in Manhattan, is credited with inventing the **Highball**. Duffy went on to publish the *Official Mixer's Manual* in 1934, a great addition to any cocktail book collection, with editions released in 1940, 1948, 1955, and 1956.

1896: Per Conrad's *The Martini*, we learn that the first published recipe for the likely predecessor to the Dry Martini appears in Thomas Stuart's *Stuart's Fancy Drinks & How to Mix Them*, specifying the use of Plymouth Dry gin. The recipe, at the time known as a **Marguerite Cocktail**, was fashioned from two-thirds Plymouth gin, one-third French vermouth, and a dash of orange bitters.

ALSO: Jennings Cox, an American engineer working in Cuba, mixes local rum with sugar and fresh lime juice, henceforth known as the **Daiquiri.** In subsequent years, Admiral Lucious Johnson introduces the Daiquiri to the United States through the Washington D.C. Army and Navy Club. Constantino Ribalaigua, who presides over the famous La Floridita in Havana, Cuba from 1912–1952, is widely recognized for advancing the Daiquiri's popularity, and for creating its frozen version.

1897: The Waldorf-Astoria Hotel opens as the largest hotel in the world. According to *The Old Waldorf-Astoria Bar Book,* by Albert Stevens Crockett, barman Johnnie Solon creates the **Bronx**—named for the zoo, not the borough.

LATE 1890s: The American Bar opens at the Savoy, London, one of the first to serve uniquely American "cocktails." Naming a bar an "American Bar" was a common practice in Europe to advertise the sale of American cocktails.

MEANWHILE, DOMESTICALLY: San Francisco's legendary bartender Duncan Nichol created the **Pisco Punch** at the Bank Exchange. Locally, it was to become one of the most popular drinks of the era.

1900: Colonel James E. Pepper claims credit for creating the **Old Fashioned** at the Pendennis Club in Louisville, Kentucky. There is much debate on where the drink actually originates—and even more on how it should be mixed.

1911: According to *Harry's ABC of Mixing Cocktails*, the "New York Bar" opens in Paris on Thanksgiving Day, at 5 Rue Daunou. Harry MacElhone is hired as the first bartender but left as WWI arrived and went on to work in New York and later at Ciro's Club in London, where he published his book in 1919. Harry returned to Paris in 1923 and took over his previous house of employ, calling it "Harry's New York Bar," as it remains to this day.

ALSO: The first **Dry Martini** (equal parts London Dry gin and Noilly Prat vermouth, with orange bitters), is mixed at the Knickerbocker Hotel in New York…by head bartender Martini di Arma di Taggia. This is supported by John Doxat in his book, *The World of Drinks and Drinking*, which promotes the notion that this was the first true Dry Martini.

1912: Absinthe is declared illegal in the United States. Portrayed as both dangerous and addictive, this powerful elixir's "harmful effects" were most likely a result of its extremely high proof—45 to 75 percent alcohol by volume. (Having consumed many an **Absinthe Drip**, I have yet to hallucinate or see the Green Fairy.) Fortunately, honest absinthe is once again available for constructing such classics as the **Monkey Gland** and the **Corpse Reviver #2**.

1915: Ngiam Tong creates the **Singapore Sling** at the Long Bar inside Singapore's Raffles Hotel. According to historian Ted Haigh, "the Singapore Sling was created in or around 1915 in the Long Bar probably under the original name of the Straits Sling, renamed officially the Singapore Sling some time between 1922 and 1930."

1916: The **Aviation** is credited to Hugo Ensslin, bartender at New York's Hotel Wallick and author of *Recipes for Mixed Drinks*. "One of the last truly great cocktails to be invented before Prohibition," states David Wondrich in his book, *Imbibe!*, and I would have to agree.

PROHIBITION: 1920-1933

Once during Prohibition I was forced to live for days on nothing but food and water.
　　W.C. FIELDS

The Golden Age abruptly concluded in 1920 with the advent of Prohibition. Among other disappointments, Prohibition, also known as the Volstead Act, stripped domestic bartenders not only of their jobs but also their profession. The one positive note, as Grimes reflects in *Straight Up or On The Rocks*, was that in the era to come, "Woman civilized the saloon, not by closing it down, but by ordering their drinks alongside men." Thank goodness for that.

It's widely believed that many classic cocktails came out of the Prohibition era, but with a few exceptions this wasn't the case. Perhaps the most famous was the **Alexander**, a blend of gin, crème de cacao, and cream; this one, perhaps fortunately, did not survive repeal. Most bartenders armed themselves with just about anything they could find in order to cover up or mask the taste of bad distillate: canned fruit, fruit juice (mainly orange for making **Orange Blossoms**), cream, honey, and corn syrup, to name a few. You can imagine the results. Hence the finer enduring drinks of this era are overwhelmingly attributed to barmen working in Europe and London.

1921: Pete Petiot first mixes his famous **Bloody Mary** at Harry's New York Bar in Paris. Pete continued to work at Harry's until the repeal of Prohibition in 1934, when he was lured back to New York's St. Regis Hotel to take the helm at its famous King Cole Bar. Harry MacElhone and the New York Bar are also credited with creating the **White Lady** and the **Sidecar** around this time—though Harry Craddock, of the American Bar in London's Savoy Hotel, has also been credited with creating the White Lady.

1920s: Another seminal cocktail of the era (and my personal favorite) is the **Negroni**, an aperitivo, first mixed by bartender Fosco Scarselli at Casoni, a café on Italy's famous Via Tombabouni. This epic cocktail was named for Count Camillo Negroni, perhaps the drink's original and most avid admirer.

1925: The **French 75,** named for the French 75 millimeter cannon used in the first World War, comes out of Harry's New York Bar. Known for packing a kick, it first appeared in print in Harry Craddock's *Savoy Cocktail Book*, but ultimately found popularity at New York's Stork Club during the 1930s. The **Mimosa**, another champagne-based recipe, emerges from the hands of Frank Meier at the Ritz in Paris that same year.

1931: Harry's Bar opens in Venice, Italy. The story is that Giuseppe Cipriani, a bartender at the Hotel Europa in Venice, lent 10,000 lire to a financially strapped Yank named Harry Pickering. Pickering eventually repaid Giuseppe's generosity (along with a hefty interest payment) and proposed they open a new establishment together. Harry's went on to become the home of the exquisite **Bellini**.

REPEAL: 1934-1969

With the repeal of Prohibition, the bar was once again open for business. America was suffering in the throes of the Great Depression and many were eager to self-medicate through drink. Things get off with a bang in 1934, one of the most significant years in cocktail history.

1934: Cocktail culture begins to gain momentum in earnest. *Esquire* magazine publishes its list, "The 10 Best Cocktails of 1934," recounted by Grimes, in *Straight Up or On The Rocks*: the **Old Fashioned**, the **Dry Martini**, the **Ward 8**, the **Daiquiri**, the **Vermouth Cassis**, the **Champagne Cocktail**, **Planter's Punch**, the **Old Fashioned Dutch**, the **Harvest Moon,** and the **Vodka Cocktail**. *Esquire*'s list is notable for the appearance of vodka—still a fairly little-known spirit in the United States—as a recipe feature, a landmark development in American cocktail consciousness.

ALSO: Donn Beach, formally Ernest Raymond Beaumont Gantt, opens Don's Beachcomber bar in Hollywood. He later opened Don the Beachcomber restaurant in 1937, pioneering the tiki craze in the U.S. He is perhaps best known for creating the **Zombie**.

ALSO: Victor Bergeron opens his first restaurant and bar, called Hinky Dinks, on the corner of 65th and San Pablo in Oakland, California. Likely influenced by the growing popularity of the tiki theme, in 1937 Vic exchanged his restaurant's sportsman décor for one of Polynesian whimsy—hence—Trader Vic's was born.

ALSO: Russian émigré Rudolph Kunett acquires the rights to produce Smirnoff vodka in America, setting up shop in Bethel, Connecticut. Ironically, since Prohibition's repeal—and Americans' new freedom to forgo inferior bathtub gin in favor of quality English Dry gin— there was little enthusiasm for Kunett's newly introduced, "odorless, tasteless" spirit. He eventually sells his small distillery for $14,000 to John G. Martin, an executive for a little company called Heublein. Needless to say, vodka's day would eventually come.

1937: My own most important cocktail milestone: my cousin, Helen David, and her mother open the Brass Rail Bar in Port Huron, Michigan. The bar opens on June 15, 1937, and Helen remains until her death in 2006. She was a strong woman, and the first person to put a cocktail shaker in my hand.

1944: "Trader Vic" Bergeron creates his famously enduring **Mai Tai**. In a creative mood, he mixes 17-year-old J. Wray & Nephew rum, fresh lime juice, sugar, orange curaçao, and orgeat syrup. Vic recounts in his *Bartenders Guide* that he presented the new concoction to two visiting Tahitian friends, who proclaimed "*Mai tai roa áe!*"—meaning, "Out of this world, the best."

1946: Vodka continues to struggle in popularity. At this point, John G. Martin, along with Jack Morgan at his Los Angeles restaurant, the Cock 'n' Bull, decides to develop a new drink. Morgan had been trying, unsuccessfully, to market a spicy ginger beer to his customers. Teaming with another friend eager to off-load a gross of copper mugs, Martin and Morgan create a drink of Smirnoff vodka, fresh lime juice, and ginger beer, calling it the **Moscow Mule**.

1954: Rum returns to the mainstream in such drinks as the **Piña Colada**—attributed to the Caribe Hilton in San Juan, Puerto Rico.

1967: For the first time, more vodka is consumed than gin in the United States.

THE SPRITZER YEARS: 1969-1985

This era was less than memorable for the American bartending profession, with little more to be said from the consumer perspective. The hand-crafting of cocktails nearly disappeared from view, taking a back seat to artificial, pre-made mixes and white wine spritzers. Classics such as the Martini and Manhattan fell from favor. High-octane, "more-must-be-better" concoctions became the rage, such as the Long Island Iced Tea.

In lieu of squeezing juices and shaking fresh cocktails, bartenders were dispensing Margaritas from frozen drink machines. (This perhaps explains why so many consumers still don't have an authentic point of reference for this wonderful drink.) Even in New Orleans, birthplace of the cocktail, frozen daiquiri bars became commonplace, dispensing premade concoctions with no more resemblance to a Daiquiri than Dairy Queen has to Italian gelato.

This was a tough time for those among us eager for a well-crafted libation, a pleasure that was fast becoming invisible as a civilized social pastime. The "Happy Hour" was embraced with cult-like fervor. Bar owners were busy, and happily cultivating their almighty bottom line.

1970s: The **Harvey Wallbanger** is supposedly named after a fictional character, Harvey, who wiped out in a surfing competition, then drowned his sorrows in Screwdrivers topped with Galliano—the cumulative effects of which influenced him to bang his head against a wall.

1974: Baileys Irish Cream is introduced, and becomes an important part of such drinks as the **Orgasm, Screaming Orgasm, B-52,** and **Mudslide.**

1976: Vodka surpasses whiskey to become the most popular spirit in the United States. It has yet to look back.

LATE 1970s: The **Long Island Iced Tea** we are familiar with today is created by Robert "Rosebud" Butt.

1984: DeKuyper introduces Peachtree Schnapps, leading to a frenzy in the flavored schnapps world. The **Fuzzy Navel** (peach schnapps and orange juice) becomes all the rage, driving the sales of Peachtree Schnapps to over 1 million cases in its first year.

1985: Wine coolers take off, with Bartles & Jaymes leading the pack.

1985: The peach schnapps wave continues to roll with the introduction of the **Woo Woo** and the **Sex on the Beach.**

THE RESURGENCE OF THE COCKTAIL: MID-1980s TO PRESENT.

Ask any of us old-schoolers and the milestones will differ, but in general our sense of the classic cocktail's comeback is likely to be fairly similar. In my personal experience, 1985 seemed to signal the pendulum's swing back toward classic.

There are of course many pioneering professionals who have played an integral part in resurrecting the appreciation of well-made cocktails. Many of these have heavily influenced my own professional sensibilities, helping me shape my own creative approach to crafting cocktails from a foundation of classic barmanship and culinary creativity. Happily, the resurgence continues to gain strength, as still more wonderful bars and bar professionals have gained prominence—each providing a serious nod to the classic era.

1985: In San Francisco, I discover places like Jack Slick's Balboa Café, where the bartenders, decked out in starched white jackets, squeeze juice fresh daily and make Ramos Gin Fizzes from scratch—egg whites and all. A nod must also go to Jack's brother, Norman Hobday, who in a sense never really experienced the resurgence in classic cocktails, for he never made cocktails any other way. Norman ran many great cocktail bars in San Francisco, including Henry Africa's, where I believe the first **Lemon Drop** was made.

1987: Restaurateur Joe Baum entrusts Dale DeGroff with running the newly remodeled Rainbow Room atop Rockefeller Plaza. Challenged with realizing Joe's dream—creating a bar reminiscent of the nineteenth-century Golden Age—DeGroff featured classics made exclusively with fresh ingredients and no mixes. Through his passionate dedication to quality, DeGroff has become widely recognized as the single most influential force behind the modern revival of American cocktail culture today.

1988: Bix is founded by Doug "Bix" Biederbeck at 56 Gold Street in San Francisco. When you ordered a **Sidecar** from barman Bradley Avey, you couldn't help but feel it was prepared the way Harry MacElhone would have made it.

1990s: Great Britain has a longstanding, undeniably talented, and ambitious cocktail community, with London serving as its epicenter. Dick Bradsell, perhaps best known for his work at the Atlantic Bar & Grill and for creating the **Bramble,** is a driving force in London's cocktail scene. Over the years he has been involved in several successful London bars.

1994: Colin Field takes the helm at the Bar Hemingway in the Ritz Hotel in Paris. His book, *The Cocktails at the Ritz Paris*, is one of my favorites. I've enjoyed several trips to the Bar Hemingway, and none was more memorable than when Colin himself prepared for me a **Ritz 75**, their twist on the classic French 75.

1995: Harry Denton reopens the historic Starlight Room atop the Sir Francis Drake Hotel. Although not a bartender per se, Harry has done more than most to revitalize lounge culture, from the opening of his namesake establishment on Fillmore Street in the 1980s, to his glamorous Harry Denton's on Stuart Street.

2000: Sasha Petraske opens the "member's only" Milk & Honey on New York's Lower East Side.

2003: Julie Reiner opens her art deco-inspired Flatiron Lounge in Manhattan's historic

Flatiron district. She follows that up with Brooklyn's **Clover Club** in 2008.

2005: Salvatore Calabrese opens Salvatore at FIFTY in London. A modern-day legend among barmen, he has to this point published eleven books, including his best-selling *Classic Cocktails*.

2006: Audrey Saunders pays homage to a British officers' club in creating **Pegu Club** in New York's SoHo. In San Francisco, **Bourbon and Branch** opens, located in what had been an actual speakeasy. Both establishments—like the Clover Club—are named after classic drinks.

Mixology Basics: Building Cocktails

PREPARING GREAT MIXED DRINKS requires that you learn the basics that are fundamental to the craft. Among these are the basic tools required to make drinks, and the basic techniques to get good results. Remember, we're not talking here about just throwing something together according to a simple recipe—we're talking about what's involved in getting better results: drinks that taste better and look better because they're prepared better. Here's what you need to know—the basics of mixology.

BAR TOOLS AND HOW TO USE THEM: THE BASICS

Bar tools are the equipment and devices used to prepare drinks. As with so many other kinds of tools and devices, it's easy to go overboard in the barware department.

I always look for high quality when selecting barware—although this generally translates to higher prices. You get what you pay for, as is so often the case; high-quality tools will often last you many years. Aside from ensuring they're well made, be sure your tools feel good in your hands. These are tools, after all, and thus they should be user-friendly and built to perform. They are also, for many of us, objects to be admired—though that's not a primary consideration.

There are numerous specialized items that you can explore further if you wish, once you master the basics. I recommend that you acquire these essential items to get you started:

▶ Boston Shaker

The Boston shaker is actually a two-piece set, consisting of a 16 ounce (480 ml) mixing glass and a slightly larger 26–28 ounce (780–840 ml) mixing tin. If you were to stock your home bar with only one piece of barware, it should be the Boston shaker. I use this versatile shaker to prepare most every drink mixed by either shaking or stirring. Many of you will be more familiar with the looks of the three-piece, or Cobbler shaker—which is, admittedly, much easier to use. However, I strongly recommend getting comfortable working with a Boston shaker—it really does a much better job of mixing and chilling your ingredients.

▶ Barspoon

A long-handled barspoon is crucial for cocktails that need to be stirred rather than shaken. The long handle allows, with a little practice, for you to spin the spoon between your thumb and fingers.

The back of a barspoon can be used to layer a drink such as a Pousse Café. It can also be used as a teaspoon (5 ml) measure.

▶ Hawthorn Strainer

This is the strainer most commonly used behind the bar, featuring a spring-like coil that fits securely in the mixing tin of your Boston shaker. Drinks that are shaken should be strained from the mixing tin through the Hawthorn strainer.

▶ Julep Strainer

This strainer has a concave body with holes and no spring. It's designed to fit in the mixing glass of a Boston shaker set with the concave side facing down. Whenever a drink calls for stirring, it should be prepared in the mixing glass and strained using the Julep strainer.

▶ Muddler

This is similar to the pestle of a mortar and pestle set, and used to extract flavor from fruits and herbs. Invest in a good-quality, natural hardwood muddler that's 8–10 inches long—enough to reach the bottom of any mixing glass. Be careful not to buy a lacquered or varnished version, as the finish will eventually wear off into your drinks. Treat your muddler as you would any wooden cooking tool: never wash it in the dishwasher, but rather clean it with mild dish soap and warm water, and allow it to air dry. It will last longer if you treat it with food-grade mineral oil on occasion.

Citrus Juicer

Preparing great drinks means using a lot of fresh-squeezed citrus juice, so if you don't already own a citrus juicer, you need one. Either an electric or a hand-operated juicer will work fine, according to your preference, but whichever you choose, make sure it's of good quality and has the capacity to juice all types of citrus.

▶ Jigger

This classic two-sided measuring device is similar in shape to an egg cup. A jigger has a larger side, also called a jigger, which measures an ounce and a half (45 ml), and a smaller side, called a pony, that measures an ounce (30 ml). Jiggers come in other sizes, but this one is the most popular. I highly recommend the use of a jigger; you have to measure out the ingredients in order to make a well-balanced drink.

Knives

Bartenders, home or professional, should own good knives and make sure they are always sharp. Be sure you have the right knife for the job. I recommend having three:

- a four-inch paring knife, used for slicing detail garnishes
- a serrated knife for cutting citrus fruits
- a chef's knife for prepping larger fruits such as pineapples and melons

▶ Lime Squeezer (Hand Juicer)

A hand-held lime squeezer is invaluable for ex-

tracting fresh lime juice at the moment you are preparing a drink. Lime is the most fragile of all citrus juices. Ideally, you should squeeze it just before use. Not only will you be assured the freshest juice possible, but you will also capture the rind's wonderful oil-based aromatics. In a pinch, a large hand juicer can accommodate lemon halves as well, though I prefer using a citrus juicer (see above) for lemons.

MORE BAR TOOLS: THE ADVANCED COLLECTION

Once you've acquired the items listed above, you might want to think about broadening your mixology toolkit. While they may not be essential for getting things off the ground, I believe you should consider getting the following tools as your mixing dexterity expands.

Bar Blender

Every household should have a good blender. It's essential for making Piña Coladas, frozen Daiquiris, and Brazilian Batidas—not to mention the legendary Funky Monkey (page 125). There are many great blenders available. I personally like those made by Hamilton Beach and Vita-Mix.

Cherry Pitter

It's very specialized, yes. But this device is a huge time-saver when preparing cherries used for mud-dling in drinks, creating Bing cherry-infused rum, or whipping up a batch of brandied cherries.

Citrus Stripper, Zester, or Channel Knife

This is a crucial tool for cutting fresh lime, lemon, or orange spirals (twists) for garnish. It may seem simple to use, but channel knives and strippers require a little practice to master. Once mastered, you'll probably consider it one of your essential mixology tools.

Corkscrew

The sky is really the limit when it comes to corkscrew options. In general, I say stick with what you like to use. The opener referred to as a Waiter's Helper is my personal favorite, and it's simple to use. The winged corkscrew, which drills into the cork, is my least favorite; I find it's almost guaranteed to tear the cork of that favorite bottle you've been saving.

Cutting Board

Invest in a good-sized rubber-composition cutting board and reserve it solely for your drink preparation needs. (In other words, don't use it for chopping garlic or onions.) I recommend owning a few in different sizes. I would start with two: one that is large enough to accommodate more sizeable fruits like pineapple and watermelon, and a smaller one that's more suitable for preparing garnishes and other ingredients.

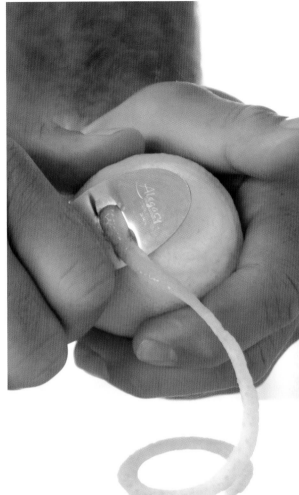

Grater

Whenever a drink calls for nutmeg, you should always grate it fresh into the mixing glass, or to "dust" the drink, such as you would with a Milk Punch. Certain graters, such as those made by Microplane, will also allow you to grate chocolate and citrus zest. These are extremely sharp tools, so be careful to keep your fingertips and knuckles away from the grater surface.

Ice Pick

For those who appreciate a great whiskey served over ice, try making or buying a large block of ice and chipping off relatively large cube-sized chunks. This is the way ice was originally used behind the bar, and with a little practice, you can impress your friends with such commitment to detail. With a steady hand, an ice pick can also be used for removing the rind from citrus fruits to make twists and spirals.

Ice Scoop

You never want to handle the ice when making drinks for your friends. There are many, many different shapes and sizes of ice scoops, so select one that meets your personal needs. I'd start with a 6-ounce (180 ml) scoop, which is 4 inches (10 cm) deep by 2

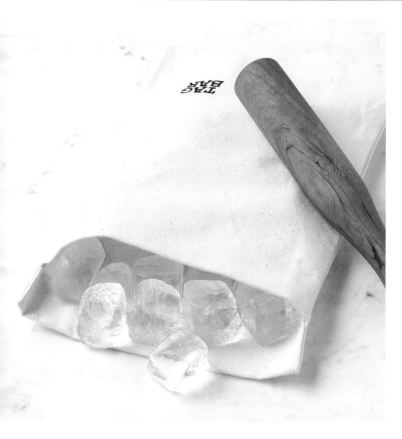

Lewis Bag

This vintage piece of barware, which was used to crush ice prior to the invention of the ice crusher, is still a valuable tool for those of you who may not own a refrigerator that generates crushed ice. Place a large amount of cubed ice in this heavy canvas bag, place the bag on a hard surface, and strike it with your muddler, or a rolling pin, until you achieve the desired amount of crush. (Of course, this can also help you relieve the anxieties of a long and stressful day!)

Melon Baller

Handy for making great-looking garnishes for tropical drinks.

Measuring Spoons and Cups

Measuring cups generally come in a set: ¼, ⅓, ½, ⅔, and 1 cup (60, 80, 120, 160 and 240 ml respectively). A set of measuring spoons range from ⅛, ¼, ½ and 1 teaspoon (0.6, 1.2, 2.5 and 5 ml respectively), as well as ½ and 1 tablespoon (7.5 and 15 ml respectively). If you don't already have a good set of both, these are a good investment for the long run. Remember, mixology is more like baking than free-hand cooking—accurate measuring is essential for consistency.

Mixing Beaker

For cocktails that require stirring, I prefer a glass beaker that is lipped and holds approximately 20 ounces (600 ml). This allows for plenty of ice cubes and enough spirit to make two cocktails. The 16-

inches (5 cm) wide. And if you find you need it, go for the next size up, 12 ounces (360 ml), or 6 inches (15 cm) deep by 3 inches (7.5 cm) wide.

Juice Extractor

This tool is a must for preparing fresh juices other than citrus. Depending on your zeal for including fresh juices in your recipes, you may soon find that a juice extractor is one of your essential tools. Try fresh-pressed pineapple, watermelon, grape, or apple juice. It will also come in handy for savory drinks, as you can use it to create a vegetable juice for your own Bloody Mary-inspired recipe.

ounce (480 ml) mixing glass that accompanies the tin in a Boston shaker set can also be used for any drink that requires stirring.

Seltzer Bottle

These bottles are used for drinks of the "fizz" style—those calling for the addition of seltzer water. If you don't want to use commercial seltzer, you can make your own by using one of these. Again, for the person truly committed to showing attention to detail. The brand I prefer to use is called iSi.

Squeeze Bottles

These plastic bottles, such as those used for dispensing condiments, can come in handy for storing and dispensing your own homemade sugar syrups, fresh fruit purées, and fruit coulis. They come in a wide variety of sizes. I recommend starting with 10- (300ml) and 20-ounce (600 ml) capacity bottles.

Swizzle

Traditionally, a swizzle was a long branch that ended in a trimmed root cluster of four or five small branches. A modern day swizzle resembles a miniature egg-beater with a very long handle. The use of a swizzle is called for when you are making a Swizzle—a drink made with crushed ice. Shaking such a drink would over-dilute its ingredients.

Tea Strainer

Drinks that require muddling to incorporate such ingredients as fresh berries or savory herbs will ben-

efit from being strained through a fine sieve or tea strainer prior to serving. This is known as double straining. A tea strainer can also be used to dust a mint sprig with powdered sugar.

Three-Piece Shaker (Cobbler Shaker) ▼

This consists of a body, which is where the drink is prepared; the top, which has a built-in strainer; and the cap, which covers the strainer. Look for a shaker that accommodates at least 16 ounces (480 ml) so you can make at least two cocktails at the same time. Invest in a sturdy shaker made from sterling silver, silver plate, pewter, or stainless steel.

Tongs

There are two types of tongs, each for a different use. The first would be a larger set intended to handle cube ice, a nice touch to accompany an ice bucket when serving a spirit on the rocks or in a Highball. The second would be a smaller set of tongs intended for handling garnishes.

Vegetable Peeler

I have been known to use the vegetable peeler for creating garnishes when a channel knife (citrus zester) isn't handy. It is also useful for making larger citrus peel garnishes.

Food Processor

A processor is always a luxury but it will come in handy when making fresh fruit purées. I am a fan of Kitchen Aid, but there are a lot of great brands available. If you don't have one, though, you can accomplish similar results with a good bar blender.

MIXING METHODS: THE BASICS

I taught you everything that you know.... But I didn't teach you everything that I know!

Helen David

To shake or to stir? That is indeed the question... The cardinal rule is if the drink contains spirit only—the Manhattan for example—it should be chilled through stirring. Cocktails that contain spirit as well as mixers—e.g., the Daiquiri, with its lime juice and sugar—should be shaken. I make an exception for the Vodka Martini, which I will shake, though I will always stir a traditional Martini made with gin. Regardless of preference, bottom line, mixing cocktails requires learning specific techniques.

Shaking

To shake a cocktail using a Boston shaker, you start by adding the cocktail's ingredients to the mixing glass, and then filling the mixing tin two-thirds full with ice. Then pour the ingredients from the mixing glass to the ice-filled mixing tin. Place the mixing glass securely into the mixing tin at a very slight angle, sealing them together tightly by striking the bottom of the mixing glass twice firmly with the heel of your hand. You should then be able to pick up the

entire Boston shaker by the mixing glass, without the seal breaking. You're ready to shake.

Shaking styles vary by individual. The next time you are at a bar, watch your favorite bartender work his or her personal style. You may want to start by grasping the tin in one hand and securing the glass with the other. Be sure to hold your shaker with the tin positioned forward, away from you. Don't be shy when working your shaker. As Harry Craddock wrote in the classic *The Savoy Cocktail Book*, "Shake the shaker as hard as you can: Don't just rock it: You are trying to wake it up, not send it to sleep!" Give the shaker at least 10 to 15 seconds of vigorous shaking for best results. Remember, you are not only chilling the drink; you are also ensuring that all of the ingredients are fully integrated.

Once your drink is mixed and chilled sufficiently, break the shaker's seal by holding the shaker with one hand, tin down, with two fingers placed on the glass and two on the tin. Then hit the top of the tin where it meets the glass, briskly, with the palm of your free hand. This frees the glass to be pulled up and away from the tin. Strain the drink from the mixing tin using your Hawthorn strainer, into your glass of choice.

Remember, you should shake drinks that include any additional ingredients besides straight spirit. Any drinks that include bubbly ingredients like champagne should be rolled.

Stirring

Remember, you will want to stir any drink that is made up of spirit only—for example, a Negroni (page 148) or Manhattan. Stirring a cocktail requires the use of the mixing glass portion of a Boston shaker set and a long-handled barspoon. Start by filling the glass three-quarters full of ice, preferably large cube ice. Add the spirits to the ice-filled glass. Slide the back of your barspoon down into the glass and stir, gently, twirling the stem of the barspoon between thumb and first two fingers. How long is best to stir? I stand by Helen David's advice: "Stir 20 times to the right and 20 times to the left." Once it's properly chilled, strain the drink from the mixing glass, using a Julep strainer, into a cocktail glass.

Rolling

Rolling is the preferred technique for preparing drinks made with tomato juice, such as a Bloody Mary, which need to be mixed without shaking (shaking would emulsify the juice and change the drink's texture). This technique should also be applied when mixing any fizzy ingredients, such as prosecco in a Bellini (page 120). (You never want to shake any type of carbonated beverage. Do, and you will have a small explosion on your hands.) To roll, use both parts of your Boston shaker. Fill your mixing tin three-quarters full with ice, add the rest of the drink ingredients to the mixing glass, then gently "roll" the drink from glass to tin and back again, several times, until sufficiently mixed and chilled. Strain the drink from the mixing tin using your Hawthorn strainer.

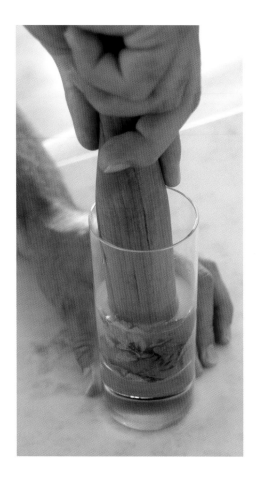  

▲ Muddling

This technique is used to extract juice and essential oils from fruit and herbs. Using a muddler and a glass (as you would a pestle and mortar), very gently massage the fruits and/or herbs with the business end of the muddler to release their flavors. You don't have to pulverize them, just release their juices and/or essential oils.

▶ Double Straining

This is an important step to remember whenever you want to remove unwanted ingredient particles from your drinks. Double straining is done after the muddling and/or mixing of your drink, but before it finds its serving glass. Use this technique, for example, when you muddle ingredients such as fresh berries, fruits, or herbs but do not want any of the particulate, such as seeds, leaves, or pulp, to be in the final drink. To double strain, the drink is poured from the mixing tin with a Hawthorn strainer in place, into and through the tea strainer, directly into its serving glass. This technique gives you a clean drink with all the flavor of the muddled fruit or other ingredients intact. The Cesar Ritz (page 170) and the 323 (page 87) are both cocktails that are double strained in the preparation process.

Blending

Although I don't make many frozen drinks, there are better ways to get good results when making them. When a drink calls for blending, always add the liquid ingredients to the blender first, and then add the ice. And you should always try to use cracked or coarsely crushed, as it will give your drink a smoother consistency and will save wear and tear on your blender.

Building

When the word "build" appears in the preparation instructions for a drink, it simply refers to making a drink in the glass within which it will be served. Generally, the ingredients are added in the order listed in the recipe. A perfect example of building is the Highball, where you add ice to a glass, followed by your spirit of choice, top it with soda, then stir, garnish, and serve with a swizzle stick.

Layering

This technique is used for building drinks such as the Pousse Café or B&B. This style is usually prepared in a pony glass (measuring 1 ounce or 30 ml) by floating or layering one ingredient on top of another. Depending upon the density of the ingredients (spirit, liqueur, syrup), you will end up with distinct ingredient layers filling the glass. Spirit density can generally be determined by the alcohol and sugar content: the less alcohol and more sugar, the heavier the ingredient, and vice versa. Start with the heaviest liquid. Pour gently down the back of the bar spoon. This directs the liquid rather specifically to wherever the bowl of the spoon is placed in the glass. Gradually add the next ingredient or layer, pouring each gently over a barspoon held just above the layer below, in order to minimize disturbance of the under layers. The trick is to keep the layers from mixing with each other. This drink-making skill is great fun to perfect and sure to impress your guests.

Swizzling

This singular mixing technique is reserved for preparing the style of drink called a "Swizzle"—a drink made with crushed ice. It helps the spirit react with the crushed ice, while avoiding the over-dilution

that would occur with shaking. The swizzle is placed between the palms of your hands with the forked, or beater, end placed in a pitcher or glass filled with crushed ice and other ingredients. It is then rotated between the palms, as though one were attempting to start a fire with dry leaves and a stick.

GLASSWARE: THE BASICS

Take the Martini. Its mere mention conjures a deeply distinct image—its glass, a shape that is timeless, elegant, and evocative of drinks culture as a whole. As William Grimes puts it in *Straight Up or On The Rocks*, "The triangular glass with an olive in it has been adopted as the international symbol for the bar." What would the Martini become without its iconic vessel? No telling, but it's safe to say that the entire experience would be inextricably altered were it served in a can.

I am one of many who believe that the resurgence in classic cocktails is due partly to our affection for the elegant glassware in which they are served.

As far as I am concerned, glassware does make a difference. This is one of the most overlooked, yet crucial components of any bar. According to Bill Kelly in *The Roving Bartender*, "Saloonmen used to take pride in their glassware. Before Prohibition, it was common to enter a bar that mixed a drink for 12 ½ cents and drink it from a glass that cost $6 or more per dozen." In many of today's establishments, attention to glassware has floated toward the opposite end of the cost spectrum.

Consider the proper serving vessel as though it were an artist's canvas. Taking particular care with

1   2   3   4   5   6

presentation will indeed improve the overall experience. The touch and feel of a glass in your hand, its size, balance, and appearance, all make their impression and therefore are an important part of enjoying a great cocktail. Just remember, don't skimp on quality. A Martini just tastes better from a thin-rimmed crystal glass—I am convinced! It may seem elitist, but the truth is I will avoid ordering a Martini from any establishment that pays inadequate attention to glassware.

Aside from its aesthetics, a glass's shape can influence the overall taste experience. Where cocktails are concerned, how the nose (in addition to the taste buds) experiences flavors is intimately tied to the shape of the glass. Think of kicking back some red wine from a tumbler; it will work, of course, but it's not exactly the same experience as when it is sipped from the properly shaped vessel. I recommend a few essentials for getting your personal collection and mixology adventure underway:

Cocktail Coupe (1)

Sometimes known as the "Marie Antoinette coupe" or "champagne saucer," this shallow, broad-bowled glass is making a bit of a comeback. I personally like to use this glass for cocktails that contain juice, cream, egg, or syrups along with spirits.

Cocktail Glass (2)

What's a cocktail glass? Think Martini. Ever since the late 1980s arrival of the Martini craze, virtually anything served in a cocktail glass was referred to as a "Martini" of one kind or another, and since then, the glass has been known better by that name. In truth, there are countless versions of the cocktail glass. In my opinion, the classic rendering is a true work of art, but to each their own. I do think, though, a few rules should be followed when selecting a cocktail glass. First, it should be stemmed. Warm hands should never touch the cold bowl of a cocktail glass. Second, there is the question of size. For the record, a cocktail glass shouldn't be more than 6 to 7 ounces (180–210 ml) in size. (With that in mind, the cocktail recipes in this book are formulated for serving in glasses of this size.) The original Martini would have been served in a glass of 3 or 4 ounces (90–210 ml) at most. In the words of Harry Craddock in his *Savoy Cocktail Book*, "A cocktail should be short, and snappy" and it "should be consumed quickly while it's laughing at you!" I completely agree. No one needs to drink a 12-ounce (360 ml) Martini. Treat your cocktail glass with respect. Wash it properly, buff it with a linen towel, never handle it by the rim, and always chill before allowing it to greet your cocktail.

Old Fashioned Glass (3)

The Old Fashioned is the namesake vessel for this classic drink. Look for a glass with good heft, a solid shank (bottom), and a capacity of 10 to 12 ounces (300–360). In addition to Old Fashioneds, this glass will serve you well when serving Caipirinhas, Sazeracs, and the Blackberry Press (page 101), as well as any straight spirit served on the rocks.

Highball Glass (4)

The Highball, a simple blend of spirit and mixer served over ice, is best served in this tall, narrow glass of 10 to 12 ounces (300–360 ml). This shape will help prolong the life of a drink with a carbonated mixer such as soda water or ginger ale. Choose a glass that feels good in your hand—and yes, it should ideally match the design of your Old Fashioned and Collins glasses.

Collins Glass (5)

Slightly taller and narrower than the Highball glass is the Collins glass, with a 12- to 14-ounce (360–420 ml) capacity. This is used primarily for the Tom, John, and entire Collins family.

Goblet (6)

You'll notice many of the recipes found within these pages call for a Goblet. It should be footed, with a bulb-like shape and a 14-ounce (420 ml) capacity. It is perfect for housing a Margarita Primo (page 143), Sunsplash (page 166), or Zig Zag (page 186).

SPECIALIZED GLASSWARE: THE ADVANCED COLLECTION

Whether you decide to explore a little further with presentation, or you want to stay true to serving a drink in its ap-propriate intended vessel, consider the following to add to your collection:

Whiskey Sour Glass

This footed glass with a 3- to 5-ounce (90–150 ml) capacity is the traditional glass for serving Whiskey Sours straight up. It can also be used to serve port, sherry, madeira, and liqueurs.

Fizz or Delmonico Glass

This is a 6- to 8-ounce (180–240 ml) glass, not un-like a smaller Collins glass, except with a slight V-shape to its bowl.

Brandy Snifter

Despite its name and popularity, this is not actually the best glass for experiencing brandy. Its large surface area allows the alcohol to concentrate, and thus overpower the subtleties of a fine cognac. Better to serve it in a small, tulip-shaped glass; these are also excellent for sipping aged rums and premium tequilas. Though I don't recommend them, I admit there is something about the vision of Dad sitting in front of the fireplace with a big snifter of brandy that's just too precious to resist. Whichever you choose, make sure you never warm it before pouring the brandy; it should be warmed gradually by the heat of one's own hand grasping the bowl.

Champagne Flute

Perfect not only for enjoying fine bubbly, but also any champagne-based cocktails; try the Champagne Celebration (page 111). Here again, think elegance—think crystal.

Shot Glass

These can range from 1-ounce (30 ml), or pony size, to 1.5-ounce (45 ml) jigger size. Shot glasses are generally used for consuming spirits neat, and all too often, in a hurry.

Heat-Tempered Glass

If you are a fan of Hot Toddies and/or coffee drinks, this glass is a must. Look for something with a stem and a capacity of 7 to 8 ounces (210–240 ml).

ICE

Ice was jewelry, only the rich could wear it.
MARK TWAIN

Ice is perhaps the single most overlooked ingredient in drinks preparation, yet one of the most important. Nothing will ruin a great cocktail faster than bad ice. "Bad ice?" you may ask. Can there be such a thing? Stop and consider...

Friends are invited for the evening and Martinis are on the menu. You have purchased several different styles of gin, a selection of vodkas, even premium French dry vermouth. Through no small effort, the Spanish olives are now stuffed with Maytag Blue cheese, sun-dried tomatoes, smoked almonds, or anchovies, for the less timid. There are a dozen
unchristened crystal cocktail glasses chilling in the freezer. You even popped for the crystal Martini pitcher.

The vision—treat your guests to a magnificent Martini, complete with selection of witty garnish. Your doorbell rings, guests arrive, canapés are presented. You steal away, eager to produce the first round. As you open the freezer door, it dawns on you ... you forgot the ICE!

Tucked at the back of the freezer, you spot an old aluminum ice tray that should have been tossed years ago, now partially obscured by a passel of frozen fillets from last summer's fishing trip. A quick rinse with hot water and the freezer fuzz is removed. It's less than ideal, but it will have to do.

Into the pitcher clinks the ice, then the vermouth and gin, and then the mixture is stirred until well chilled. Before long the contents are carefully strained into the delightfully frosted glasses. With stuffed olive garnish and linen napkin in tow, the look is nothing short of perfection.

First sips are taken while you anxiously await murmurs of approval. Their eyes rise from the first sip to meet yours with an expressiveness that can only convey, "Eau de salmon?" Enough said.

The take-home message: always use fresh ice. It absorbs aromas and flavors from freezer-mates, and will quickly become stale. At the very least, ice

should be made within a week of serving. Further, bad water yields bad ice. If you live in an area where the water is very hard and contains lots of unpleasant minerals, use bottled water in your ice tray. And by all means, toss the old aluminum war-horse and splurge on a nonmetallic device that will not impart flavor to your ice. For the culinary elite (and resource flush), a reverse osmosis filter system connected to your icemaker is a fine addition. For the rest of us, there is always the option of buying ice. Just be sure to buy enough; the last thing you want is a cocktail party stalled by an ice shortage.

If making your own ice, here is another tip; having practiced various methods to produce the clearest, hardest, coldest possible homemade ice, I have found a method that works very well. Bring bottled water to a boil, pour it into ice molds (I prefer to use silicone moulds of a larger cube size), then immediately place these in your freezer. My theory is that when I start with boiling water, the ice freezes slower and yields a clearer cube.

This may seem obvious, but the truth is, ice should be hard—simply, very well frozen and thus more "dry." Your goal is maximum chill and minimal dilution; wet ice melts faster, and in turn will water down (cocktail professionals use the term "bruise") your cocktail. For example, consider the perfect Dry Martini: it should consist of approximately 20 percent water, derived of course from ice. Soft ice equals a too-weak Martini. Also, you should never, with a few explicit exceptions, use the same ice to serve a drink as was used to prepare it.

So, what kind of ice is best? Cubes, cracked, or crushed … does it really matter? Yes—different grades of ice are appropriate for different kinds of drinks.

- **Cubes**—This is the best selection for spirits to be served "on the rocks" or in a Highball. Remember to use larger cubes, as these will melt more slowly and keep the drink colder longer without as much dilution. Cube ice is also recommended for use in preparing both shaken and stirred cocktails; remember, your goal is maximum chill, minimum dilution.

- **Cracked**—Best reserved for blender drinks. Cracked ice won't place the same strain on your blender as cube ice. Prepare it by placing cube ice in a Lewis bag or a linen napkin and beating it lightly with a mallet or rolling pin. The Lewis bag or napkin will absorb any water that melts while the ice is being cracked. This is also the correct ice for the very rare drink—such as the Caipirinha—in which the ice served with the drink is the same ice used in its preparation.

- **Crushed**—There are several grades of crushed ice, ranging from a coarse crush, for Mojitos or Juleps, to a fine snow-like crush for a Mist or a Frappé. Both are made by leaving cracked ice in a Lewis bag or napkin and abusing it with a mallet or rolling pin until you achieve the desired consistency.

Take good care in making and handling your ice—remember, it's an important element of your cocktail.

FOLLOW THE SEASONS—SPIRIT AND FLAVOR PAIRING

Live in each season as it passes: breathe the air, drink the drink, taste the fruit.

Henry David Thoreau

Mixology, in essence, is about finding the most harmonious and pleasing flavors to pair with spirits. To that end, I believe that if you think and drink (and mix) seasonally, you can take best advantage of the incredible assets handed you by Mother Nature. Consider the variety of seasonal fruits, vegetables, and herbs, and imagine the vast range of flavors available to you. Have a look the next time you're in your local grocery, or search out whatever specialty markets are near you. You will find plenty of creative options. True, many fruits are available year-round in frozen form. For my part, though, I like to operate from more of a *carpe diem* frame of mind. Seize the day, and live—and therefore drink—for the moment!

For me, little compares to a vine-ripened Michigan strawberry, picked right at the peak of freshness. Take full advantage of what your part of the world has to offer from one season to the next. At their seasonal summer peak, for example, consider creating something with beautiful, ripe Bing cherries. Try infusing them into rum for a twist on the Daiquiri or Mojito, or muddle them with fresh lime, simple syrup, and cachaca in a Caipirinha. Or think about setting them aside in brandy, to be savored in a Manhattan when the weather turns gray once again.

Spirits: The Basics

When combining fruit or savory flavors with spirits, there are certain principles you should follow, at least loosely. For instance, a fresh, ripe raspberry that marries happily with gin or citrus vodka may not work well with a rye or Scotch whisky. In turn, those wonderful apricots we are blessed with in the summer months will be the perfect complement to bourbon whiskey or nicely aged Jamaican rum. Many good combinations will become apparent to you as a result of trial and error, so you need to do a lot of tasting in order to discover what works best for your palate.

A good way to start is to review each spirit category, and learn more about pairing them with other ingredients; in particular, I want to share with you some of my knowledge about fruit-spirit pairings—and savory-spirit pairings—that I find work nicely together. Again, this is only a basic road map. Feel free to experiment with combinations that appeal to you. It may take some time, but rewards will abound when you discover a great-tasting new cocktail. I will add one key dictum that applies across the board: always remember that in mixology, balance is paramount.

Brandy

Brandy, a sixteenth-century Dutch creation, is essentially made from fruit and can be divided into three distinct categories—those distilled from wine, pomace (the solid pulpy remains of grapes used in making wine), or other fruits (such as apples, pears, or cherries). When mixing drinks, you should think of using cognac, or any of the fine domestically produced boutique brandies. You may also want to consider apple brandies such as calvados from the Normandy region of France, which are derived from hard cider. You may already have your own established favorites in all of these subcategories, so by all means try them out. I have created drinks with a pretty wide variety of brandies ranging from Hennessy VS cognac, to domestic brandy produced by the Germain-Robin Distillery in California, to Laird's Applejack, to name just a few.

All brandies are fruit based, so they tend to mix well with a wide array of fresh fruits. Since cognac is made from wine, grapes are a natural pairing. I would choose a seedless variety—white, purple, or red—and use them either muddled or juiced. As cognac's intense flavor becomes more concentrated with age, it also mingles well with dark tree fruits such as plums, pluots, and figs. Try blueberries and fresh lemon juice with a touch of sugar for a unique variation of a Brandy Sour. In general, I am not inclined to pair brandy with savory ingredients, though I am sure it has been done.

When working with calvados or applejack, both match up wonderfully with tree fruits: pear, cherry, apple, and pomegranate, to name a few. I also sometimes use these apple-based brandies as a substitute for when traditional cognac is called for—in the

Sidecar, for example—or as a base spirit for a ginger- or unfiltered apple juice-themed cocktail.

Gin

The gin we know and love today is a descendent of a spirit called genever, which originated in sixteenth-century Holland. Its characteristic flavor is primarily that of juniper, enhanced by a variety of other botanicals and/or spices—the combination of which is, of course, proprietary from one brand to another. Hence, the vast differences among gin flavor profiles.

The more traditional style of gin, associated with the "London Dry" or "masculine" style, is much more heavily flavored with juniper. Many newer brands are much more citrus-forward in taste and aroma. Bombay Sapphire is a wonderful example of these newer, softer, "feminine" gins, whereas Tanqueray would be the quintessential juniper-forward style. A third flavor profile is that of Plymouth gin, which I consider to be of a style all its own—a well-rounded, fruity flavor that rests somewhere between the other two. Naturally, the only way to know for sure how best to work each one's strengths is to taste, taste, taste.

One of my all-time favorite pairings is gin (particularly a feminine-style brand) with raspberries. Gin also works well with fresh citrus juice, such as lemon and lime, of course, but also things like Ruby Red grapefruit and blood orange. The botanical flavors in certain gins—such as orange and lemon peels, cinnamon, and anise—work nicely with green and yellow melons like honeydew and casaba. I would also suggest you try kiwi, lychee, or the winter citrus fruits—clementine, honey tangerine, and Meyer lemon. As for savory options, cucumber, mint, and basil are worthy of consideration.

Rum

Rum (sometimes spelled *rhum*) is primarily identified with the Caribbean, though technically it can be produced elsewhere. It's made from sugar, generally either molasses or the fresh-pressed juice of the sugar cane. Rum comes in endless varieties, from light bodied to heavier, more complex rums, not to mention a breadth of spiced and flavored rums. There is a rum out there that will pair well with nearly any fruit imaginable. With rum, more than with any other spirit, it's important to taste it in order to identify and consider its flavors.

Light-bodied rums work well with subtle ingredients, such as fresh lime and spearmint, that generally do not stand up to heavier rums. Melon—honeydew, casaba or Crenshaw—is also a great match when made into a purée. Cherries, whether infused in rum itself or muddled in a seasonal Mojito, are delicious in combination with a lighter rum. When you want to try making your own infusions, I find light-bodied rums work best—they will pair well with just about anything you want to experiment with. Bacardi Superior and Cruzan are both solid examples of good light-bodied rums.

Complex rums with multiple layers of flavor are generally complemented by flavors found in the rum itself, such as coconut, banana, apricot, and mango. Consider blueberries muddled with fresh wedges of lime and a touch of raw sugar. Ginger and vanilla bean are also wonderful choices. A couple of good examples of this rum style include Mount Gay Eclipse and 10 Cane.

Heavy, full-bodied rums will stand up to powerful tropical fruits such as papaya, mango, passion fruit, and guava. Few pairings rival rich Jamaican rum with fresh pineapple juice—simple and divine. Apricots also hold up exceptionally well against a heavier rum. Both Myers's and Appleton are good examples of full-bodied rums.

Cachaca, sometimes referred to as Brazilian rum, is distilled from 100 percent sugar cane juice. It is best known for its appearance in the traditional Brazilian drinks, the Caipirinha and Batida. I also use it in my Banana Shaker (page 93). Cachaca flavor profiles can range from raw, rowdy, and aggressive to smooth, refined, and elegant. I like both Leblon, which is considered an artisanal cachaca, and Pitu, which is more on the industrial, or lively, end of the category spectrum. It matches up well with most citrus, especially those winter fruits—kumquat, clementine, Meyer lemon, and blood orange. You could also add berries along with one of the citrus fruits for an additional layer of flavor—blue-, black- and raspberry will all hold up well. Savories such as basil, sage, or mint also work well.

Tequila

Tequila conjures more myth, legend, and lore than perhaps any other spirit. Once considered a less refined item, premium tequila now sits firmly on the shelf with the finest of all distillates. It's hard to generalize about what works best with 100 percent agave tequila, as its flavor profile differs dramatically with age—from blanco, to reposado, then onto añejo. The agave's growing region lends it even further subtleties—highland versus lowland, that is.

Blanco (silver) is aged no longer than 60 days, and it's full of clean, fresh agave flavor and aroma. It can be earthy but also full of fruit, spice, and floral tones. This category is truly the best representation of the agave plant. In a mixed-drink recipe, think of pairing blanco with lighter citrus such as lemon, lime, orange, and tangerine, and stone fruits, such as nectarines, plums, and pluots. For going savory, think of peppers and chilies, even hibiscus or lavender. Both Tres Generaciones, a lowland-based distillery, and El Tesoro, from the highland region, produce excellent blanco.

Reposado (rested) is aged in wooden containers, of any type or size, for a minimum of two months up to one year. The fruit, floral, and spice notes of the agave will be more apparent, with hints of vanilla and caramel from the wood. Apricots, guava, Rainier cherries, and any of the berries are a good match for reposado's features. I also favor Ruby Red grapefruit. Patron is a great highland reposado; from the lowland region, I like Partida.

Añejo (aged) is tequila that has aged for a minimum of one year in oak barrels. Think of the unique character of rich caramel, huge vanilla, cream soda, and toasty oak, paired with complex fruit and spice textures, and you're in añejo's territory. This richest of tequilas goes great with pomegranate, apple, blood orange, quince, prickly pear, and ginger. Siete Leguas produces an exquisite highland añejo, and Herradura is well known for its lowland version.

Whiskey

What can you say about whiskey, and the vast range of its different varieties? There are American, Scotch, Irish, and Canadian versions, each the product of a unique ancestry and distillation process. I tend to use the American whiskies in my drink recipes. It's probably best to consider the three American whiskies separately: bourbon, rye, and Tennessee. Though similar in style, each will contribute a slightly different taste and character to the finished drink.

Bourbon is distilled from a mashbill, a specific recipe of combined grains. Each producer's mashbill recipe is unique, but is made from a combination of corn, malted barley, and either wheat or rye. Virtually any stone fruit will be a natural pairing with bourbon—peaches, apricots, plums. You may also want to experiment with pluots. A great example of a ryed bourbon is Jim Beam Black Label. For a wheated bourbon, think Maker's Mark.

Rye is best known for its bold, spicy tones; consider summer tree fruits, such as yellow peaches, apricots, and nectarines. A tamarillo, muddled or puréed, and Bing or Rainier cherries will all lend amazing flavor to a rye whiskey. For its mixability, I really like (ri)1—pronounced "rye one."

Tennessee whiskey and its big, sweet smokiness go great with fresh-pressed apple juice and apple cider, especially when you heat it up and add some cloves and cinnamon sticks. I also think citrus—Meyer lemon, tangerine, kumquat, blood orange—as well as pears. Try making and using cinnamon-stick simple syrup as an accent for added depth and complexity. Only two distilleries produce Tennessee whiskey: George Dickel and Jack Daniel's.

Blended whiskey—whether American or Canadian—is best suited for a Highball. You will also find it used in a Whiskey Sour or John Collins. Blended whiskey's light, sweet, almost lightly honeyed layers are simple, approachable, and highly mixable. For a twist on a Sour, try tangerine, blood orange, clementine or Meyer lemon. Seagrams 7 is a representative American blend; for Canadian, Crown Royal is a good choice.

Irish whiskey, for the most part, is best enjoyed neat, over ice, in a Highball with ginger ale or club soda, or in an Irish Coffee. It does have a particular sweetness that lends itself to persimmons, the plum family, ginger, pears, and apples. You might try either Jameson's or Bushmill's, but I also like the lesser known Powers.

Scotch whisky (note the slightly different spelling unique to Scotch) is probably the most difficult kind of whiskey both to pair with fresh fruits, in particular, and to use in creating mixed drinks in general. I recommend that you steer clear of experimenting with those prized single malts and focus your attention more on blended Scotches like Cutty Sark, Dewar's, and Chivas Regal. Search out the blends made primarily of Highland malts, as these tend to be more floral and fruity. Once you have found a blend you like, consider trying fresh fruit variations on drinks like the Collins or Sour. Dark fruits such as Bing cherry, blackberry, and blueberry will absolutely shine. Don't overlook the citrus category; blood orange, tangerine, and clementine will all work very nicely, as will kumquat when muddled with lemon and sugar.

Vodka

Vodka's popularity is in large part due to its infinite mixability.

Take virtually any fresh fruit juice—say, Ruby Red grapefruits—add vodka, and you have a libation (in this case, the delicious Greyhound). Try experimenting with some of the more uncommon fruits like feijoas, lychee, persimmons, or pummelos (and of course anything from the citrus family). For those who enjoy a savory tilt, consider tomatoes, cucumbers, ginger, sage, peppers, lavender, hibiscus… Honestly, the list goes on and on and on.

It should be no surprise that vodka is the easiest spirit to pair with both fresh fruits and savory ingredients, as vodka by definition is meant to be tasteless, colorless, and odorless. That said, there are indeed nuances particular to the region of the world in which a given vodka is produced, subtle though they may be. Finlandia is an approachable, western

European vodka. Stoli is the classic example of Russian-style vodka; and both Belvedere and Chopin are exemplary of the Polish style.

Flavored Vodka

This is where things get a little more interesting, vodka wise. Of course, you'll need to balance your selected pairing flavor with that of the vodka. This may not sound difficult, but consider the vast number of flavored vodkas on the market, not to mention the proprietary variation within each category. Some will work better for your palate than others. Taste and evaluate its underlying nuances first, then you can decide which flavors will work best in complement. Although there are a large number of different flavors produced, the most common (and highly mixable) are citrus/lemon, orange, vanilla, and raspberry.

Citrus/lemon vodka is a safe bet mixed with any citrus fruit. Blackberries and raspberries also work beautifully, as do plums and nectarines. A ripe kiwi, peeled and puréed, is also a great complement. One of my favorites is fresh-pressed watermelon juice—don't let their size intimidate you, as they are packed with flavor and natural sweetness when in season.

Orange vodka works well with most citrus juices, or muddled with blood oranges, kumquats, and clementines in the winter months. It also works well with more exotic fruits such as guava and passion fruit.

Raspberry vodka works well with any kind of berry. Also try lemon or Meyer lemon for a tasty citrus/berry balance, or puréed casaba melon.

Vanilla vodka should inspire you to step a little outside the norm. Coconut, banana, chocolate, almond—try them all together, or one at a time. Also, papaya, lychee, passion fruit, strawberry, and apricot are all great ideas, too.

INFUSION JARS

Infusions have become a popular way of imparting that little extra *je ne sais quoi* into a cocktail. You create an infusion by allowing a select ingredient—fruit, spice, vegetable, or herb—to soak in a quantity of spirit for a prescribed period of time. Generally, it might take a week to create an infusion, but you can certainly experiment with different infusion times to taste. The flavor profile of any classic spirit can be transformed through this process, but vodka, with its relatively neutral flavor, remains the most popular option.

Whatever fruits, vegetables, spices, or even peppers or chilies you select for infusing, the same basic principles apply. The key to a great infusion—no surprise—is to select the freshest, ripest, best ingredients. There is of course no reason to limit the selection to just one—combining a variety of ingredients can produce delightful results. I like to think the delight is in the experimentation as much as in the consumption, so just go for it. In the case of a hot, fiery chili-based infusion, be warned…it may be

prudent to start with a conservative amount, lest the final concoction overpower. Of paramount importance: the infusion jar must be made of glass only, and feature a mouth wide enough for the easy placement and removal of ingredients.

Go-To Fruit Infusion

One of my favorite infusions is a layered combo of pineapple, strawberries, blueberries, and vanilla bean. Start with a clean wide-mouth jar, add a layer of skinned, cored, and sliced ripe pineapple, then a layer of sliced strawberries, followed by blueberries, and finally a vanilla bean that's been sliced lengthwise with seeds exposed. Continue layering until the jar is three-quarters full. Next, cover the fruit completely with vodka, saving any empty vodka bottles for later use. Seal the jar with a lid and store in a cool place for five to seven days, or until the flavor and sweetness of the infusion is to your liking. When you are happy with the taste, strain the liquid back into the clean, dry vodka bottles. The resulting infusion can be stored in the refrigerator for up to a month. You can enjoy your infusion over ice, or shaken and served in a chilled cocktail glass, or you can use it to create a twist on the classic Cosmopolitan.

Chili Pepper Infusion

Yes, chili peppers. From the temperate Anaheim and poblano, to the more intense green and red jalapeños—within the chili family, temperatures range from mild to scorching, so do your research as to which will suit your palate best. Every time I make

this infusion it is with a different mix of peppers, dictated both by what is available and by what looks good—and yes, the results are indeed quite different with every batch.

Once you've selected your chilies, rinse them thoroughly and prick them several times with a pin. Fill a wide-mouth jar three-quarters full with assorted chilies and cover completely with vodka. Cover and infuse for five to seven days, depending on the heat level you are seeking, and then strain off the liquid into clean, dry bottles before storing in the refrigerator for up to one month. My recipe for the Blond Mary (page 102) calls for this infusion, but it will also add a kick to a classic Bloody Mary, the Bloody Bull, the Bloody Caesar, or any savory creation of your own.

Bing Cherry Infused Rum

Embrace summer's fleeting cherry season. Take fresh Bing cherries and rinse them thoroughly, making sure to exclude any bruised or overly soft fruit. Remove their stems. This next step can be a little messy, so do yourself and your clothing a favor by wearing rubber gloves and an apron, and use a good cherry pitter. Remove the pits and place cherries in a clean, wide-mouth jar until it is three-quarters full of fruit. Cover completely with light-bodied rum, seal, and store in a cool place for 7 to 10 days to infuse. Strain the rum back into the clean, dry rum bottles, seal, and store in your refrigerator for up to a month. Your Bing cherry rum is now ready for use: this infusion is delicious in a classic Mojito, a classic Daiquiri, or anything you want to create of your own.

Homemade Limoncello

An infusion of sorts, this limoncello is in fact a homemade liqueur. Limoncello is readily available for purchase, but easy to create on your own. The process is very simple, but requires a certain amount of patience—with two distinct and lengthy resting periods—but in my experience it's well worth the wait. Select 20 good-sized lemons with thick yet smooth skins; you'll only be using the outermost portion of the skin (though you can save the lemons for juicing). Rinse lemons in warm water and clean them thoroughly with a vegetable brush. Use a vegetable peeler to peel only the yellow skin (and none of the white pith) from the lemons. Place peels in a clean, wide-mouth one-gallon jar and cover them completely with two 750 ml bottles of Everclear—(you may substitute 100 proof vodka if you prefer). Place the jar in a cool, dark place for 45 days. Give the jar a shake every couple of days. After 45 days, filter the alcohol through a fine sieve and cheesecloth to remove the lemon peels, then return it to your gallon jar.

The next stage requires the addition of a sugar syrup. Bring 7 cups (1680 ml) of water to a boil, and into it dissolve 5 cups (1200 ml) of sugar. Allow your syrup to cool, then add it to your lemony alcohol, reseal the jar, and give it a good shake to mix. This step both sweetens your liquor and dilutes the high-proof Everclear. Place the jar back into a cool, dark place to rest for another 45 days. When ready, transfer your limoncello into clean, sealable bottles and store in your refrigerator until needed.

The classic way to enjoy limoncello is neat, from a frosted shot glass taken straight out of the freezer—the perfect digestive after a wonderful meal. I use it in both the Serrano Cocktail (page 160) and the Blackberry Press (page 101), but I also recommend it as a modifier in a tequila-based drink.

Rosemary Infused Gin

Gin is the perfect canvas for infusions toward the savory end of the spectrum. My recommendation, since no two gins are created equal, is that you first evaluate your favored gin's flavors, then chose an herb, vegetable, or spice that you feel will provide the best compliment. I am fond of Hendrick's with its hints of cucumber and rose petal, as a match for fresh rosemary. Take a large sprig of rosemary, rinse it thoroughly, and place it in a liter bottle of gin. Set it aside in a cool dark place for five to seven days, then remove the rosemary sprig. Store it in the refrigerator and use within a month. The end result is tried and true in my repertoire, and I worked it into my 323 cocktail (page 87). It would also add a wonderful layer of flavor to a Red Snapper (gin Bloody Mary). Cucumber, basil, and strawberry are all flavors I think of pairing with this infusion.

Serrano Infused Tequila

Try spicing up tequila with your favorite chili. I like using silver or unaged tequila with serrano chilies.

Add 3 to 4 chilies to a liter of tequila. Pierce each chili with a pin, before placing it in the bottle. Place in a cool, dark place for a month, shaking the bottle occasionally. When ready, taste to test for heat and spice—if you'd like it hotter, let it infuse a few days longer. This adds a really nice zing to a Bloody Maria or straight up with a Sangrita chaser.

Vanilla Bean Infused Vodka

Making your own vanilla bean infused spirit is an easy substitute for purchasing commercially produced vanilla vodka. Simply slice a vanilla bean lengthways to expose the seeds inside and place the bean in a 750 ml bottle of your favorite vodka. Store in a dark, cool place for up to a week, or until the vodka has taken on as much vanilla flavor as you prefer. Remove the vanilla bean, reseal the bottle, and store in the refrigerator for up to three months. Don't be afraid of the little black specks; they simply show that you infused your own vodka with a real vanilla bean. Use this infusion when making a Vanilla Gorilla (page 178) or in a simple twist on a Vanilla Coke.

Rock & Rye

Think of this as a rye-based whiskey liqueur. Rock & Rye is an elixir once cherished for what were believed to be its medicinal properties. It's a yummy alternative to straight rye, and it makes a fine modifier or accent. It can be purchased, but it's difficult to find, so I make this version and use it when I make a Spiced Cider Toddy (page 162). This recipe ap-

peared in *The Gentleman's Companion*, published in 1946 by Charles H. Baker, Jr.:

Rye whiskey, ⅕ gallon, not a full quart

Jamaican rum, jigger

Rock candy, ½ cup, leave in large lumps

Whole cloves, 1 dozen

Quartered small California orange, peel left on

Quartered seedless lemon, peel left on

Stick of cinnamon, or two

Put ingredients in jar, cover with rye, and let stand for a fortnight (2 weeks). Strain out spices through fine cloth or filter paper. Put back on fruit until needed.

SELECTIONS BY SEASON

There really are so many more pairing options or considerations than I could reasonably describe here. I offer this seasonal-pairing chart to provide you with further inspiration.

Ingredient Selections by Season

legend   B—Brandy   R—Rum   V—Vodka   (YR—Year-Round)

             G—Gin   T—Tequila   W—Whiskey

FRUIT	SEASON	PREPARATION	SPIRIT(S)
Apricots	June–Aug	Purée	R, W
Anaheim Peppers	YR	Infuse, muddle	T, V
Asian Pears	YR	Juiced, muddle	G, V
Blackberries	YR (best May–Oct)	Muddle, infuse	B, R, V
Blueberries	YR (best June - Aug)	Muddle, infuse	B, R, T
Bing Cherries	June–July	Purée, muddle	B, R, W
Blood Oranges	Dec–June	Juice, muddle	G, T, V
Cantaloupe	YR (best June–Sept)	Purée	G, R, T
Cape Gooseberries	Aug–Oct	Garnish	
Casaba Melon	June–Sept	Purée	G, R, T
Champagne Grapes	July–Oct	Garnish, muddle	B, G, R
Cherimoya	YR	Purée	R, T

FRUIT	SEASON	PREPARATION	SPIRIT(S)
Cinnamon	YR	Infuse	R, T, W
Clementine	Oct–Dec	Juice, muddle	G, R, T
Clove	YR	Infuse	R, T, W
Cocktail Grapefruit	Nov–Feb	Juice	G, T
Coconut	YR	Milk, garnish	G, R
Concord Grapes	Aug–Sept	Juice, muddle	B, V, W
Crab Apples	Winter	Garnish	
Cranberries	YR (best Sept–Dec)	Muddle	G, R, V
Crenshaw Melon	June–Sept	Purée	G, R, T
Cucumber	YR (best May–Aug)	Muddle	G, T, V
Feijoas	April–Oct	Purée	G, R, V
Figs	July–Sept	Muddle	B, W
Galia Melon	June–Sept	Purée	G, T, V
Grapefruit	Oct–June	Juice	G, R, T, V
Green & Red Jalapeño	YR	Infuse, muddle	T, V
Guava	YR	Purée	R, T, V
Hibiscus (dried)	YR	Infuse	B, G, R, T, V
Honey Tangerine	Jan–March	Juice, muddle	G, R, T

FRUIT	SEASON	PREPARATION	SPIRIT(S)
Honeydew	YR (best June–Sept)	Purée	R, T, V
Kaffir Lime	Dec–March	Juice	G, V
Key Lime	YR (best June-Aug)	Juice, muddle	G, R, T, V
Kiwi	YR (best June-Aug)	Purée, muddle	G, R, V
Kumquat	Dec–June	Muddle	G, R, V
Lychee	June–Sept	Purée, muddle	G, T, V
Lavender (dried)	YR	Infuse	G, T, V
Meyer Lemon	Nov–May	Juice	G, R, T, V
Nectarine	May–Oct	Muddle, purée	B, R, W
Nutmeg	YR	Garnish, spice	R, T, W
Page Mandarin	Dec–Feb	Juice, muddle	G, T, V
Papaya	YR	Purée	B, R
Pasilla Pepper	YR	Infuse, muddle	T, V
Passion Fruit	Jan–July	Purée	B, R, T
Peaches	May–Sept	Purée	B, W
Persimmon	Sept–Dec	Purée	B, R, W
Plums	May–Sept	Muddle	B, G, W
Pluot	June–Sept	Muddle	B, W

FRUIT	SEASON	PREPARATION	SPIRIT(S)
Pomegranate	Aug–Oct	Infuse, juice	G, T, V
Poblano Pepper	YR	Infuse, muddle	T, V
Prickly Pears	Sept–April	Purée	R, T, W
Pummelo	Nov–March	Juice	G, T
Quince	Sept–Dec	Bake & purée	B, R, T, W
Rainier Cherries	June–Aug	Muddle, infuse	R, W
Rambutan	Aug–Feb	Garnish	
Rosemary	YR	Infuse, muddle	G, T
Seedless Grapes	YR (best July–Oct)	Juice, muddle	B, G, V
Serrano Pepper	YR	Infuse, muddle	T, V
Star Fruit (Carambola)	YR	Garnish	
Strawberries	YR (best May–Sept)	Muddle, infuse	G, R, T
Tamarillo	May–Oct	Purée	B, R, T, W
Tangerine (assorted varieties)	Sept–March	Juice, muddle	G, R, T, V
Tomato	YR (best May–Aug)	Juice	G, T, V
Vanilla Bean	YR	Infuse	B, R, W
Watermelon	YR (best June–Sept)	Juice	G, V
White Peaches	June–Aug	Purée	B, G, W

MIXERS & GARNISHES

Mixed drinks might be compared to music; an orchestra will produce good music, provided all players are artists; but have only one or two inferior musicians in your band, and you may be convinced they will spoil the entire harmony.

WILLIAM SCHMIDT,
THE FLOWING BOWL

Remember, when it comes to cocktails, the quality of the final product is a sum of all of its parts. Mixers and garnishes are an enormous part of a proper cocktail. The term "mixers" once meant pre-fab ingredient combinations to which you just add spirits, to make what I think will likely be a pretty middling drink. What you'll see

here is guidance on preparing ingredients that will bring your cocktail experience to a new level. I can't stress enough how essential it is to use fresh juices, spices, accents and other premium ingredients in assembling your cocktails.

This is particularly important when it comes to juices. There really is no substitute for using fresh juices. Few chefs would utilize a frozen or pre-packaged product in the kitchen, given the choice. Picking the right fruit or other fresh ingredient, and paying careful attention to its preparation, can make or break your drink. Learning how to pick the best produce may take some practice, but the efforts are worth the reward.

JUICES

When preparing fresh-squeezed citrus juice, always buy fruit specifically intended for juicing, such as Valencia or juice oranges. When making grapefruit juice, I always prefer Ruby Reds. With lemons and limes, look for fruit with a thin skin that is very pliable to the touch. Once purchased, never store your citrus fruit in the refrigerator—cold fruits do not yield as much juice. Also, be sure to rinse all of your fruit before use.

When you are ready to prepare citrus juice, first roll the fruit on a hard surface. This helps to release more of its juice. Just prior to juicing, slice it along its equator rather than pole to pole. Be sure to filter or strain your fresh-squeezed juice to remove the pulp and seeds—a fine mesh sieve or tea strainer works best.

As for other juices, such as watermelon, grape, apple, tomato—all are definitely worth exploring. In general, non-citrus juices are best prepared in the juice extractor. Rule of thumb: use fruits that are at the peak of their season. See what is available and go for it. There are exceptions to the "fresh fruit only" recommendation: cranberry, pineapple, and pomegranate are probably best used in the form of a reputable purchased product.

Lime Juice

Use only fresh lime juice in your drinks recipes. This is the most fragile of the citrus juices and should not be stored for later use. I also recommend you hand-extract the juice into a small container or pitcher and then measure out the desired amount. The juice of one small lime will yield approximately 1 oz (30 ml) of fresh juice.

▼ Fresh Lemon Sour

To make fresh lemon sour, simply mix two parts fresh, filtered (to remove the pulp and seeds) lemon juice with one part simple syrup. Ideally, lemon sour should be made the day you plan to use it, but it will keep refrigerated in a clean bottle for up to three days.

Homemade Lemonade

To make homemade lemonade, mix 1 cup (240 ml) fresh-squeezed lemon juice (remove the seeds but not the pulp) with 1 cup (240 ml) simple syrup and 2 cups (480 ml) cold water. Refrigerate until ready to use. It will be good for up to three days.

Apple Juice

There are so many varieties of apples to choose from, but Gala is my favorite. I recommend removing the core, stem, and seeds to avoid adding a bitter note. Once rinsed, slice the apples and put them into an extractor. Fresh apple juice should be used the same day it is made.

Grape Juice

Regardless of color, choose ripe, seedless grape varieties. Rinse them first, remove the stems, and run them through your juice extractor. Again, prepare the juice right before you want to use it; do not attempt to store freshly extracted grape juice or it will oxidize.

Tomato Juice

Pick ripe tomatoes and experiment. I recommend them all: heirloom, cherry, yellow, green, red, or a combination. Each one will give you a wonderful flavor, as long as it's ripe and fresh.

Watermelon Juice

Pick a seedless watermelon, one with a nice sheen to its skin, dark green color, and which makes a "tong tong" sound when knocked. (However, the only way to *really* know a melon's quality is to cut it open and taste it.) Once it's rinsed, cut off the rind, slice the flesh into pieces small enough to fit into the juice extractor, then juice and use the same day.

PURÉES

Purées are another great cocktail ingredient which, like juices, are best prepared using fresh, seasonal fruits. I recommend using a good food processor, but a sturdy bar blender can also do the trick. Searching out fresh frozen purées—like Boiron or Napa Valley's Perfect Purée—is also a good option.

Mango Purée

Starting with fresh, ripe mangos, I find it easiest to slice them lengthwise along both sides of the pit, yielding two fleshy mango "cheeks." Make slices on the meat of the mango against the skin. Next, using a spoon, scoop out the flesh, place it in a food processor, and blend to a smooth consistency. Be sure to taste before using; you may need to add a little simple syrup to sweeten and push the mango flavor forward. This technique can also be used for other tropical fruits, like papaya.

Pumpkin Purée

Start with a 3- to 4-pound (1–2 kg) pumpkin, cut it in half, then scrape out the seeds and threads. Place the halves, cut-side down, on a greased baking sheet. Bake the pumpkin in an oven that's been preheated to 350 degrees F (176 degrees C) for about 1 hour or until it is very tender and can easily be pierced with a fork. (You may cook it longer if you prefer it really soft.) Remove and set the pumpkin aside to cool. Once it is cool enough to handle, cut the skin off with a sharp knife. Chop the flesh into pieces small enough to fit in a food processor (or sturdy blender) and process until puréed. Pumpkin purée, in addition to being delicious, can also be refrigerated for up to five days.

White Peach Purée

Take very ripe white peaches and blanch them in boiling water for approximately one minute, then transfer them to an ice bath. Peel the peaches, remove their stones, and slice each into about five or six pieces. Transfer the peach pieces to the food processor and purée. Be sure to sample— you may need to sweeten your peach purée with simple syrup, approximately 1 oz (30 ml) per pound of peaches. If you wish, add a couple of red raspberries while puréeing to achieve a subtle pink hue. Refrigerate immediately and use within 24 hours. You can follow the same process with yellow peaches, nectarines, and apricots, minus the addition of raspberries.

SYRUPS

Syrups are a terrific way to introduce a measure of sweetness into your drinks while simultaneously imparting any number of unique flavors. You'll see that many interesting syrups can be made at home, most as basic variations on the classic "simple syrup"; however, some of the more unique flavors will need to be purchased. These are a few of my favorites, and are of course those I refer to in my drinks' recipes. Don't stop with these—be sure to experiment with creating your own.

Simple Syrup

Simple syrup is one of the essential cocktail staples—the best way to add the pure sweetness of sugar to a drink recipe. To make simple syrup, my proportion is always 1 to 1, sugar to water. Dissolve

desired quantity of sugar into the same volume of boiling water. One cup (240 ml) sugar dissolved in 1 cup (240 ml) boiling water will yield approximately 1.5 (360 ml) cups of syrup. Allow mixture to cool and store in a clean bottle in your refrigerator for up to a month.

Brown Sugar Syrup

This syrup serves as an interesting alternative to regular simple syrup, in which you swap brown sugar in for regular white sugar. I prefer using light brown sugar, but if dark yields a preferred end product, it is also fine to use. When measuring, your brown sugar should be loosely packed.

Honey Syrup

Higher on the sweetness scale than table sugar, honey adds an additional layer of complexity with various floral undertones—clover, orange blossom, apple blossom, buckwheat, heather, lavender, and so on. Prepare as you would simple syrup, substituting an equal quantity of honey for the sugar.

Cinnamon Syrup

Basically, this is cinnamon-flavored simple syrup—prepare as above, adding two cinnamon sticks to the water as you begin heating it. Remove the cinnamon sticks when cool, bottle, and store in your refrigerator for up to a month.

Vanilla Bean Syrup

Simply add half a whole vanilla bean, sliced along its length, to the simple syrup recipe, putting it into the water as you begin to heat it. Remove the bean when the finished syrup cools, bottle and store in your refrigerator for up to a month. For a more intense vanilla flavor, leave the vanilla bean in the bottled syrup.

Ginger Syrup

One of my favorites—again, a variation on simple syrup. Add a quarter cup (60 ml) of peeled and sliced ginger root to the water as you begin to heat it. This time, after you've added the sugar, return the mixture to a boil, then reduce heat and simmer it for 30 minutes. Once the mixture has cooled, remove the ginger by straining the mixture through a fine sieve, bottle, and store in your refrigerator for up to a month.

Balsamic Vinegar Reduction

This syrup-like mixture begins with 4 cups (1 L) of balsamic vinegar. In a saucepan bring the vinegar to a boil over a high heat, whisking it constantly to prevent burning. Add 1 tablespoon (15 ml) of sugar and continue to whisk until the mixture is reduced by half or takes on a syrupy consistency. Remove from heat and allow to cool. Store refrigerated for up to six months.

Grenadine

Grenadine is used in mixed drinks both as a sweetener and to give them an amazing red color. This syrup is traditionally made from pomegranates, but beware—many commercially prepared grenadines are artificially colored and flavored. If you prefer to purchase, always look for a good-quality brand, such as Angostura or Sonoma, that make their product from real pomegranates. If fresh pomegranates are available, however, I recommend you try making your own amazing version.

2.5 pounds (1.1 kg) pomegranates
1 pint (473 ml) water
Granulated sugar

Separate the pomegranate seeds from the membranes and skin. In a saucepan, cover the seeds with the water, bring to a boil, then lower heat and simmer for 5 minutes, stirring until the juice sacs around the seeds release their juice. After removing the mixture from heat and allowing it to cool briefly, pour the warm mixture through a cheesecloth-layered sieve into a bowl, pressing the juice from the seeds. Discard seeds.

Measure the quantity of pomegranate juice, return it to the saucepan, add an equal amount of granulated sugar, and heat it to a boil. Reduce heat and simmer for 15 minutes. Cool the syrup to room temperature, store it in a clean bottle with a cork stopper, and refrigerate for up to one month.

Hibiscus Syrup

This syrup has both a beautiful flavor and an intense ruby red hue, along with a strong floral sweetness.

2 cups (480 ml) granulated sugar

2 cups (480 ml) water

1 cup (240 ml) dried hibiscus flowers

Bring water to a boil and add dried hibiscus flowers. Reduce heat and allow flowers to steep for 7 minutes. Add sugar, return the mixture to a boil, then lower heat and simmer for 20 minutes. Remove from heat and allow to cool. Strain through a fine sieve and bottle. Refrigerate for up to a month.

Purchased syrups

These are more specialized items that are more challenging to produce yourself. All can add dimension to different cocktail recipes. If you're interested, you can pursue these at specialty stores or via online retailers.

Agave nectar is a very interesting natural sweetener made from the extract of wild agave. More concentrated than white sugar and featuring a unique, almost maple flavor, it comes in both light and amber varieties—amber being the more maple-like of the two. Try it the next time your cocktail recipe calls for tequila. I like to dilute agave nectar in an equal amount of boiling water and allow it to cool,

resulting in a significantly more cocktail-friendly consistency.

Cane syrup, a southern favorite, is a critical ingredient in Ti Punch. Like agave nectar, I find it works best in drinks recipes when diluted in an equal amount of boiling water, then cooled.

Maple syrup is a great sweetener with a classic flavor. This one I also dilute with the same equal-part boiling water method.

Orgeat syrup provides a subtle almond flavor and is a great addition to Polynesian-themed or rum-based drinks. Trader Vic calls for it in his Mai Tai recipe and you'll also see it used in the Golden Dragon (page 128).

Rose's Lime Juice, a syrup of sorts, was created in 1876 by Lauchlin Rose, who patented a method of preserving lime juice sans alcohol. Sweetened lime juice of any kind should not be substituted for drinks calling for fresh lime juice; however, Rose's is a key ingredient of a proper Gimlet.

OTHER MIXERS

Banana milk is made by blending two very ripe bananas with 1 pint (473 ml) of whole milk and 2 heaping tablespoons (30 ml) of powdered sugar. You can make this in advance, but it is best if used within 6 hours of preparing.

Coconut milk, not to be confused with "coconut water"—the liquid from a coconut's center—is made by mixing equal parts Coco-Lopez coconut cream with half-and-half. Refrigerate in a sealed container until ready to use.

Egg whites are the traditional emulsifier used in classic drinks including the Tom Collins, Whiskey Sour, or the American Cocktail (page 88). They are ideal for adding a creamy texture to a drink as well as a frothy appearance. If you're uncomfortable using raw egg whites, use pasteurized egg whites available at the grocery store.

Sweet tea is another traditional southern favorite that I've adapted using herbal tea (I like Celestial Seasonings Red Zinger) and honey. I use the formula of 2 cups (480 ml) of water, 2 teabags, and 2 ounces (60 ml) of clover honey. After boiling the water and removing it from the heat, add the teabags and the honey and steep for 5 to 7 minutes. Remove tea bags and let cool. Refrigerate until ready to use.

GARNISHES

True, a garnish is meant to elevate the visual presentation of a drink. However, it can also be a critical flavor element—just as important as any base spirit, modifier, or accent—contributing flavor and aroma, in addition to visual appeal. Think of the basic lemon spiral adorning the Martini. Visually, it is both simple and stunning. Looks aside, the oils released from the rind onto the drink contribute those beautiful aromatics as well as a delicate, unmistakable citrus flavor.

Not every drink needs a garnish for garnishing's sake. If it does not add to the experience, feel confident leaving a garnish out of your recipe. For drinks that are best garnished, be careful not to ignore the addition as a full-fledged cocktail ingredient.

It should be selected and prepared with the same care and scrutiny that all other cocktail ingredients demand.

Picking the right garnish starts with identifying the right fruit for the job. Remember that an orange selected for juice may not prove a good choice for garnish. Also, make sure to rinse all fruit before preparation. Last, there are certain garnishes you're better off purchasing, rather than preparing yourself.

Lemon and Lime Wedges

One of the most familiar garnishes, and one that's usually essential to the flavor of the finished drink. When a drink calls for lemon or lime juice to be squeezed into a drink—the Bloody Mary or a Margarita, for example—a lemon or lime wedge is the recommended garnish. Squeeze the wedge into the glass and then just drop it into the drink. There are five easy steps to preparing wedge garnishes:

1. First, select lemons and limes with a deep color, free of scars or bruises, heavy for their size and pliable to the touch.
2. Rinse the fruit in warm water and remove any stickers.
3. With a sharp paring knife, clip the nibs from each end of the fruit.
4. Cut the fruit in half lengthwise from end to end. Place the cut side down on a cutting board. Make two additional cuts on 45-degree angles, which will provide you with three wedges. With larger fruit, you may yield four wedges per half.

5. Remove any seeds and store covered in your refrigerator until they are needed. Only cut what you plan to use that day.

Lemon, Lime, and Orange Slices

Citrus slices are used as more of a decorative garnish than wedges, when only the aromatics of the fruit are required. I am fond of sliding a freshly cut, half-moon shaped slice of citrus into a glass rather than hanging it on the rim. Look for the use of an orange slice in the Sunsplash (page 166), and lemon slices in the Luce del Sole (page 140) and the Joy Ride (page 134).

1. Follow steps one and two as above for selecting and preparing your fruit.

2. Cut the fruit in half lengthwise from end to end. Place half of the cut fruit face down on a cutting board. Cut away one end and discard. Begin slicing in approximately quarter-inch (6 mm) slices.

3. Slice only as many as you will need that day and refrigerate until use.

Lemon, Lime, and Orange Spirals

Spirals can be cut with a citrus stripper, also known as a channel knife. Twist peels into a tight spiral, then stretch the spiral ends apart laterally, releasing the citrus oils across the surface of your drink. Another method for making spirals without the channel knife is to separate the entire rind from the fruit with a citrus peeler. Once removed from the fruit, roll the rind tight and cut it into quarter-inch (6 mm) sections; each section then becomes

a spiral. I take my Vodka Martini with a spiral of lemon, the Cable Car (page 108) is garnished with an orange spiral, and a lime spiral is the finishing touch on the Serrano Cocktail (page 160).

◀ Burnt Orange and Lemon Twists

These are a real crowd-pleaser and are not as difficult to master as you might think. Simply cut about a 1.5 inch (3.8 cm) by 1 inch (2.5 cm) disk of peel off a large, firm, thick-skinned (to assure a higher oil content) navel orange. Be sure to get just the skin and as little of the pith (the meaty white part of the orange between the skin and the fruit) as possible. Holding the orange peel between your thumb and first two fingers with its skin facing out, hold a lit match several inches above the glass. With the orange peel about an inch away from the flame, squeeze the peel quickly and firmly. When done correctly, a burst of flame will come from the oils being released out of the orange peel, leaving a wonderful aroma and adding just a note of orange essence to your cocktail. After flaming, simply place the twist in the drink. You may also want just the essence added to your drink, so feel free to leave the garnish aside, as you wish.

For lemon twists, look for a lemon with a thick, firm, yet smooth skin. Use larger lemons for flaming, as they will have a higher oil content and yield better results.

Orange and Cherry Pinwheels

Use an olive pick to combine a Maraschino cherry with an orange slice to make a pinwheel, known in the bartending world as a "flag." Wrap a cherry in an orange slice, then skewer them together. The olive pick is inserted through one side of the orange, then the center of the cherry, and finally out through the other side of the orange. This is the classic garnish for the Tom Collins and Whiskey Sour.

Mint

You always want to use mint that looks as fresh as possible. There is nothing worse than a Mojito garnished with a limp mint sprig. If the mint looks a little wilted at the market it has probably seen better days, and it's not likely to look any better by the time you start mixing drinks. Once home, rinse your mint in cold water, wrap it in paper towel, and store in a sealed plastic container in your refrigerator. Mint can be stored in this fashion for a week to ten days.

Stuffed Olives

These days you can purchase a wide variety of different kinds of stuffed olives, but even when you're stuffing your own, you still need to start by purchasing the olives. Get large Spanish olives, with or without pimentos—though of course you'll remove and discard the pimentos if present. You can stuff almost anything into an olive: blue, Brie, mozzarella, or any soft cheese; sun-dried tomatoes; fresh herbs; smoked salmon or almonds; anchovies; and roasted garlic with herbed bread crumbs. As with other garnishes, make only as many as you plan to serve. You can always keep Spanish olives on hand, stored in their own brine, for future creations.

Pineapple Spear

Vic Bergeron called for a fruit stick in his Mai Tai and I would guess he used pineapple. Using a serrated knife, cut off both ends of a ripe (but not overly ripe) pineapple. Next, cut rounds or wheels approximately 1 inch (2.5 cm) in width. Cut each wheel into 8–10 narrow spears. The pineapple leaves can also be used as a decorative garnish. Perfect for almost any tropical drink, you'll also see a spear in the Bluegrass Cobbler (page 105).

Kumquats

These little guys are fun to use as garnish and great in muddled cocktails, such as a Caipirosca. The thing to remember is that the skin is sweet and the fruit rather tart. For garnish, get creative with the paring knife and cut the skin so when you peel it back it looks like a flower.

Toasted Coconut

I love this garnish. It's so easy to make, and adds such a nice finish to drinks such as the Funky Monkey (page 125) or Vanilla Gorilla (page 178).

1. Preheat oven to 350 degrees F (176 degrees C).
2. Spread sweetened shredded coconut evenly across a baking pan.
3. Bake for 15 to 20 minutes or until the coconut becomes golden brown. It will brown from the outside of the tray inward, so you'll need to stir occasionally for even results.
4. Allow to cool and store in an airtight container.

PURCHASED GARNISHES
Olives

The standard cocktail olive for a Martini is a Spanish olive with pimento. There are different-size Spanish olives available, so follow your preference. I prefer a medium-size olive, and only one in my Martini. Unless you prefer a dirty Martini, when serving it's a good idea to remove the olives from their brine and soak them in an ice water bath for five minutes. Use them when they are cold— it is a crime to drop room temperature olives in an ice cold Martini! When storing olives, they should be completely covered in their brine, and they must be kept refrigerated.

Maraschino Cherries

Look for large, plump cherries with stems. Store them in their juice and keep refrigerated. The Manhattan is probably the most famous cocktail to be adorned with a Maraschino cherry; it's also wonderful with a brandied cherry.

Brandied Cherries

These special treats can be made at home, but they are relatively labor intensive, so I suggest purchasing them. Look for cherries that have maintained their rich dark color through the brandying process.

Cocktail Onions

Cocktail onions come in several sizes, though I prefer them a little on the larger side. This is the classic garnish of the Gibson cocktail, a traditional variation on the Martini.

Recipes...and Back-Bar Tales

DRINKS A TO Z

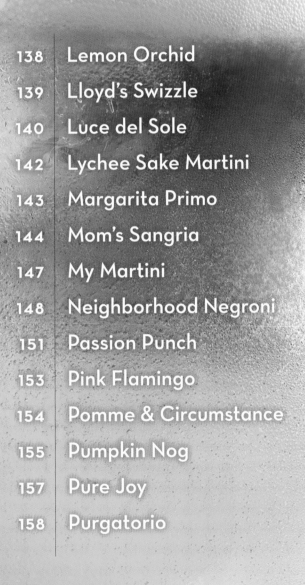

323

The bar is the grandest stage in the world and the bartender brings it to life every night!

Harry Denton

Today, I have the pleasure and honor of being in business with Jason and Joe Denton and Eric Kleinman at Inoteca Cucina, Vina e Liquori in New York City. When I designed the bar menu there, creating a seasonally fresh house cocktail naturally was high on the agenda—something aligned with our casual Italian cuisine. An apéritif, the 323 (named for the restaurant's street address, 323 Third Avenue) is intended to be enjoyed before dining, readying one's appetite for delights upcoming: sliced meats, cheeses, pasta and wine perhaps...? A little savory, a little sweet, with just the right balance of alcohol and acidity, Italian style.

Hendrick's gin, featuring cucumber and Bulgarian rose petals among its mix of botanicals, is made in Ayrshire, Scotland, and distilled in one of only four Carter-Head stills left in the world. This unique still actually bathes the botanicals in vapor, producing a sweet, lightly floral fragrance. Hendrick's provides a fine base for supporting the sweet-savory opposition among the balance of the 323's bounty of accents: fresh rosemary, fresh basil, a balsamic vinegar reduction, and fresh summer strawberries.

Here also is an example of the Modern Mixology mantra: work with the seasons! We never considered either abandoning the 323 at strawberry season's end, or using anything other than fresh seasonal fruits; in true Modern Mixology fashion, the 323 changes with the seasons: clementine, tangerine, kumquat, and blood orange all make their appearances in this drink as the year flows.

I first met Jason Denton while working for his legendary uncle, Harry, at Harry Denton's on Stuart Street in San Francisco; a superb experience, in large part because I got to work alongside some of the most amazing bartenders I've ever known. It was years later that Harry asked me to teach Jason's younger brother, Joe, to tend bar while I was at the Starlight Room. So as I look back, I say, "Thanks Harry!" for yet another ripple your stone has cast upon the waters.

2 oz (60 ml) rosemary infused Hendrick's gin

2 oz (60 ml) fresh lemon sour

½ teaspoon (2.5 ml) balsamic vinegar reduction (page 75)

2 fresh basil leaves

2-3 fresh strawberries or fresh seasonal fruit

In a mixing glass, add strawberries, basil leaves, and balsamic vinegar reduction, and muddle. Add gin and lemon sour; shake with ice until well blended. Double strain into a chilled cocktail coupe. Garnish with a strawberry half.

AMERICAN COCKTAIL

The American, by nature, is optimistic. He is experimental, an inventor and a builder who builds best when called upon to build greatly.

JOHN F. KENNEDY

This drink was created specifically for a New Year's tribute to New York City. New York—a city that is uniquely indescribable and entirely American. I wanted the drink to reflect the city's originality, sophistication, and diversity. Hence, the American Cocktail features ingredients from lands far from Manhattan's soil but integral to its heritage: rum from Puerto Rico, Maraschino liqueur from Italy, bitters from Trinidad, and champagne from France (birthplace, after all, of the Statue of Liberty). The end result—a lively, complex cocktail—was the 2003 Gold Medal winning cocktail at the Bacardi Martini World Finals in Turin, Italy.

One of the more interesting ingredients used in this cocktail is the rarely seen Maraschino liqueur, a key component in such classic cocktails as the Casino, the Aviation, and the Hemingway Daiquiri. Made from spicy Marasca cherries found in Italy and along the Dalmatian coast, Maraschino is a clear, somewhat dry liqueur that should not be confused with the fluorescent pink liquid that accompanies a jar of Maraschino cherries. To make this wonderful liqueur, the cherries are distilled much like a brandy, and the product is aged in casks of Finnish ash. The addition of a separate distillate made from the crushed stones of its fruit imparts a slightly bitter-almond flavor. This product is extremely mixable but must be used sparingly; it is very intense and very concentrated.

I am fortunate to have spent several amazing years in the great city of Manhattan, starting out in the West Village while working with Mario Batali and Steve Crane at Po. The vivid pulse of the city and its people have become a part of me.

1 ½ oz (45 ml) Bacardi Limón rum

½ oz (15 ml) Luxardo Maraschino liqueur

1 ½ (45 ml) oz fresh lemon sour

1 dash Angostura orange bitters

1 tsp (5 ml) egg white

Chilled champagne

In a mixing glass, add rum, Maraschino liqueur, bitters, fresh lemon sour, and egg white; shake with ice until well blended. Strain into a chilled cocktail coupe. Top with ice-cold champagne.

APRICOT JULEP

The mint julep is a creation that brings wisdom to fools, turns wallflowers into the life and soul of the party, makes the clumsy graceful, the weak strong, and brings sophistication and charm to the most ill-mannered lout.

GARY REGAN, *THE BOOK OF BOURBON*

Aged, yes, but by no means antiquated, the history of the Julep is traced to the very early 1800s. In William Grimes's *Straight Up or On The Rocks*, he quotes John Davis, an Englishman working as a tutor on a southern plantation, who described the Julep as "a dram of spirituous liquor that has mint in it, taken by Virginians of a morning." Originally hailed as medicinal, the refreshing basic recipe—mint, sugar, water, and shaved ice—was traditionally finished with brandy, both regular and peach. By the late 1830s only the wealthy were still using brandy, while the masses turned to whiskey, and according to Grimes, brandy eventually disappeared from the mix entirely after the Civil War, "and the bourbon Mint Julep became universal."

Fresh mint and a fine bourbon whiskey are both essential Julep elements. Sterling silver Julep cups are ideal for their superior frosting ability, but in lieu of silver, a tall 14-ounce glass will perform just fine. Remember, thinner glass facilitates the frosting process. As for the mint, only fresh, young, tender leaves will do. The Apricot Julep specifies the use of Woodford Reserve, a pot-distilled, 90.4 proof Kentucky straight bourbon, and of course fresh ripe apricots. Woodford should be familiar to horse racing enthusiasts as the official bourbon of the Kentucky Derby.

Considered the quintessential southern concoction, Juleps should be enjoyed by all who appreciate a delicious injection of frosty cool when things heat up. This drink is reserved for fresh apricot season and is one of my particular favorites for an outdoor gathering, casual or otherwise. I hope it will inspire a new wave of Julep devotees.

2 oz (60 ml) Woodford Reserve bourbon whiskey

½ oz (15 ml) Rothman & Winter Orchard Apricot liqueur

½ oz (15 ml) simple syrup

12-14 fresh spearmint leaves

3 slices of fresh apricot

Place 3 slices of fresh apricot and 12 to 14 mint leaves in each cup, add simple syrup, and gently muddle with a wooden muddler. Next fill the cup with crushed ice, add bourbon and apricot liqueur, then stir to mix. Top the cup with crushed ice, then continue to stir until a frost forms on the outside of the cup. Garnish with a "bonnet" of mint (3 or 4 sprigs bundled together). Add a straw or Julep spoon before serving to keep your guest a safe distance from the garnish. You may want to serve linen napkins with your Juleps to keep warm hands from coming in contact with the frosty cup.

BAMBOOZLE

Once I dreaded tequila but now it's all I drink. In each glass
I see sorrow; in every sorrow I see a wish.

Unknown

The Bamboozle was developed for a Hilton Hotels cocktail promotion called "Travel. Taste. Toast." Their program involved assembling a global destination-themed cocktail menu, paired with an instructional video filmed at each Hilton location represented from around the world. (I know what you're thinking—"tough gig!") This refreshing tequila-based cooler was featured for the Hilton in Cabo San Lucas, Mexico.

Two of my favorite tequila-based drinks are the Paloma, made from the simple combination of tequila and Squirt (grapefruit soda), and El Diablo, which features cassis and fresh lime juice. Drawing a bit from both—along with my love for combining a variety of citrus juices—this drink is a bit more work than your standard Margarita, but worth the effort.

Tres Generaciones tequila, affectionately referred to as "3 Gs," is a special bottling, created in the company's hundredth year of operation by Don Francisco Javier Sauza, to honor the three generations of Sauzas who have served at the helm of this venerated distillery. Their *plata* holds a wonderful citrus/spice balance that combines magically with the black currant sweetness of the cassis.

I love to travel, hitting the road with a few good friends on our motorcycles, embracing life's adventure—food and drink, and newfound friends. A wonderful way to unwind, and motivation for recognizing life's celebration wherever the road leads! I am a huge fan of the tequila category, and particularly for its highly sociable aura. The magic of this amazing spirit has delivered many a beautiful cocktail experience, but probably just as many wonderful friendships—and so often in the most surprising places!

1 ½ oz (45 ml) Tres Generaciones plata tequila

½ oz (15 ml) Marie Brizard Crème de Cassis de Bordeaux

1 ½ oz (45 ml) fresh-squeezed Ruby Red grapefruit juice

½ oz (15 ml) fresh-squeezed lime juice

½ oz (15 ml) agave nectar

Chilled lemon-lime soda

In a mixing glass, add tequila, cassis, grapefruit juice, hand extracted lime juice and agave nectar; shake with ice until well blended. Strain into an ice filled goblet. Spritz with lemon-lime soda. Stir and garnish with a wedge of Ruby Red grapefruit.

BANANA SHAKER

Never gamble with your customers, never lend money to your customers, and never, ever, date a woman you work with.

MY COUSIN, TONY ABOU-GHANEM

I have been fortunate enough to visit Rio de Janeiro and explore its legendary beaches. Leblon beach is where I happened upon the quiosque do Portugues and owner Carlos Alves, whose family has run this particular quiosque for years. There are some 300 Quiosques that line the beaches of Rio, serving light food, cold beer, Caipirinhas, and a drink locals call the Batida. Extremely popular in Brazil, the Batida is a blended drink of cachaca, condensed milk (although pretty much anything along the milk-cream continuum is used), a sweetener, and any number of fresh fruits.

A distant cousin to the Batida, the Banana Shaker—featuring crème de banana, crème de cacao, and sweet homemade banana milk—actually registers on the light side. Unlike ordinary rums, which are generally made from molasses, cachaca is distilled from fresh-pressed sugar cane juice. At around 1.3 billion liters a year in production, it's the third largest-selling spirit in the world. Leblon cachaca is produced in Patos de Minas, in the heart of Minas Gerais, Brazil. Master Distiller Gilles Merlet oversees production of this "artisanal" style of cachaca, which is distilled in alembique (copper) pot stills, and aged slightly in used XO cognac barrels.

I discovered banana milk in my early days at the Brass Rail, when my cousin Tony would make his version for me, sans alcohol. During those early years, when I was first cutting my teeth behind the stick, he would whip up a delectable banana milk that was light, fluffy, and very tasty. It wasn't until years later, though, that Tony's special banana milk occurred to me as a unique ingredient for an adult beverage.

1 oz (30 ml) Leblon cachaca
1 oz (30ml) Bols Crème de Bananes
1 oz (30 ml) Bols Crème de Cacao White
3 oz (90ml) sweet banana milk (page 76)

In a mixing glass, combine ingredients and shake with ice until well blended. Strain into a cracked-ice-filled Highball glass.

BAR FLY

Bartending may, to the man who knows nothing about it, seem a simple matter; but like everything else it is a business, and requires considerable study to become an expert.

HARRY MACELHONE, *HARRY'S ABC OF MIXING COCKTAILS*

In 1924, Harry MacElhone of Harry's New York Bar, along with an acquaintance named O.O. McIntyre, formed the International Bar Flies, or IBF—which he referred to in his book as a "secret and fraternal organization devoted to the uplift and downfall of serious drinkers. With over 130 chapters he called "Fly Traps" now established worldwide, Harry proved to be a singularly influential figure within the profession. The master behind such classics as the White Lady and the Sidecar, his book, originally published in 1919, remains an essential tool for any self-respecting barman. The Bar Fly is a concoction inspired by Harry and his fraternity of serious drinkers.

This drink features Parfait Amour, a classic liqueur from Harry's heyday. Popular with pre-Prohibition imbibers but now largely obscure, it will be recognized by fans of the classic Pousse-Café. Parfait Amour is a visually stunning light blue color, flavored with violets, oranges, and vanilla. Difficult to acquire, the effort is worth the reward. The variety produced by the Marie Brizard Company is a premier example. Marie Brizard herself started out as nurse in eighteenth-century Bordeaux. Her initial liqueur was so popular that in 1755 she formed her own company. Some eight generations later, her family still at the helm, her secret recipes remain carefully guarded.

1 ½ oz (45 ml) Tanqueray No. Ten gin
¾ oz (22.5 ml) Marie Brizard Parfait Amour
1 ½ oz (45 ml) pineapple juice
1 ½ oz (45 ml) fresh lemon sour

In a mixing glass, add gin, Parfait Amour, pineapple juice, and fresh lemon sour; shake with ice until well blended. Strain into a cracked-ice-filled Old Fashioned glass. Garnish with a lemon spiral. (If you can't find Parfait Amour, you can substitute crème de violette).

BARDSTOWN SLING

It's not about the apple, it's about polishing it.

BILL SAMUELS, STAR HILL FARM

Kentucky is known for horse breeding, bluegrass music, and world-class spirit purveyors. Bardstown, the self-proclaimed "Bourbon Capitol of the World," is home to the annual Kentucky Bourbon Festival—an extraordinary event held every September that brings all the great makers of bourbon together in celebration of this truly American spirit.

The "Sling" style of drink started off as a mix of spirits (usually gin), sugar, and water, with nutmeg grated on top. Over time it has developed into a much more complex long drink with the addition of citrus juice and liqueur modifiers. Honorable mention should go to Ngiam Tong Boon, who created the famous Singapore Sling at the Long Bar in Raffles Hotel, Singapore.

The Bardstown Sling features, of course, bourbon whiskey. To find the bourbon featured in this drink one must travel just outside Bardstown, heading east to Loretto. This is where seventh-generation whiskey man, Bill Samuels Jr., can be found overseeing day-to-day operations at Star Hill Farm, producers of Maker's Mark bourbon whisky—where they spell it without the "e," just like our friends in Scotland. In accordance with the recipe developed by William Samuels Sr., Maker's Mark uses wheat rather than rye in its mashbill. With huge notes of honey, vanilla, dried fruits, and butterscotch, this 90 proof whisky stands quite soundly on its own. However, its stamina also makes it a tempting cocktail spirit, and as it happens, the perfect companion to fresh peaches—a featured ingredient in the Bardstown Sling.

Think of mixing up a few Bardstown Slings for your guests at the next weekend barbeque—it's a perfect match for spare ribs with potato salad, corn on the cob, and black-eyed peas. Should there be any fresh peaches left over after you've made your Slings, try making a peach cobbler with a little dose of Maker's Mark and a dab of Chantilly cream.

1 ½ oz (45 ml) Maker's Mark bourbon whisky
¾ oz (22.5 ml) Marie Brizard Peach liqueur
1 oz (30 ml) yellow peach purée
2 oz (60 ml) fresh lemon sour
2 dashes Fee Brothers peach bitters
Chilled seltzer water

In a mixing glass, add bourbon, peach liqueur, yellow peach purée, fresh lemon sour, and peach bitters; shake with ice until well blended. Strain into an ice-filled Collins glass. Spritz with chilled seltzer water. Garnish with a dusting of freshly grated nutmeg.

"You have to measure out the ingredients in order to make a well-balanced drink."

BAYOU ZINGER

Laissez Les Bon Temps Roullez...

This refreshing cooler features two very well-known liqueurs. The first is New Orleans's own much-loved Southern Comfort, which was created in 1874 by a bartender named M.W. Heron, who took the initiative to add fresh fruit to his whiskey—which was often rough around the edges—in order to make it more palatable. More than 125 years later, it is made in much the same fashion.

Often mistaken for a whiskey, Southern Comfort is actually a whiskey-based liqueur, with just the right balance of orange and ripe, juicy, peach flavors, perfect for building cocktails. If used as a base spirit, consider using plenty of fresh lemon juice for balance. It is the iced sweet tea that offers the "zing" in this recipe—a touch of dry against the sweet fruity backdrop of the Bayou Zinger.

Just six years younger than Southern Comfort, Grand Marnier is perhaps one of the most recognized bottles on any back bar—a delicious cognac-based orange liqueur with rich, complex citrus and floral tones. It's made with a singular Caribbean orange variety picked while still green and at its most aromatic.

The Bayou Zinger always makes me think of good southern hospitality, a plate of Chef Duke's amazing fried oysters, and a cool Bayou breeze —if there is such a thing?

1 ½ oz (45 ml) Southern Comfort
½ oz (15 ml) Grand Marnier
2 oz (60 ml) fresh-squeezed lemon juice
2 oz (60 ml) iced sweet tea

In a mixing glass, add Southern Comfort, Grand Marnier, and fresh lemon juice; shake with ice until well blended. Strain into an ice-filled Mason jar or goblet. Top with iced sweet tea. Garnish with a wedge of lemon and sprig of mint.

BLACKBERRY PRESS

I drink upon occasion and sometimes I drink upon no occasion!

DON QUIXOTE

In the mixology world, the term "Press" is often used to indicate a "Presbyterian"—a drink with no particular religious leaning, better known as a Highball mixed with equal parts soda water and ginger ale. The Blackberry Press is by no means a Presbyterian. In fact this short drink draws from both the Smash and the Sour, yet with a twist all its own.

In this case, "Press" indicates a style of drink preparation, similar to the Smash—think of the Julep or Mojito, where a muddler is used to "press" the mint against the bottom of a mixing glass, releasing the plant's essential oils into the accompanying simple syrup. With the Blackberry Press, though, the muddled products are *not* served as an integral part of the final creation, as would be the case in a Mojito. This drink's use of fresh-squeezed lemon juice calls to mind the classic Sour—traditionally recognized as a simple combination of citrus juice, sugar, and distilled spirit—in how it achieves that delicate balance between sour and sweet.

What sets the Blackberry Press further into its own category is its use of liqueurs as the spirit base. Marie Brizard Blackberry is made with freshly harvested wild fruit macerated in neutral alcohol. In addition to blackberries, a measure of raspberries, black currants, and cherries appear in the exclusive recipe for this 60 proof liqueur.

My love for limoncello, which also makes an appearance in this recipe, was solidified during a magical visit to the Amalfi Coast. Several good commercial brands are available; however, I can highly recommend the satisfaction that comes with making your own.

1 oz (30 ml) limoncello liqueur

1 oz (30 ml) Marie Brizard Blackberry liqueur

2 oz (60 ml) fresh-squeezed lemon juice

1 oz (30 ml) simple syrup

10-12 fresh spearmint leaves

4 fresh blackberries

In a mixing glass, muddle 2 blackberries, mint, and simple syrup. Add blackberry liqueur, limoncello, and lemon juice; shake with ice until well blended. Double-strain into a cracked-ice-filled Old Fashioned glass. Garnish with a couple of powdered sugar-dusted blackberries.

BLOND MARY

A blond drove me to drink, and my only regret is that I never thanked her.

W.C. Fields

If a vote were taken, the Bloody Mary would certainly be among the most tinkered-with drink recipes of all time. There are dozens of established variations, and hundreds of concoctions wearing the same iconic name. As it happens, the Bloody Mary came to us from across the pond after the repeal of Prohibition, and has led a winding journey ever since. The original recipe, created in 1921 by Pete Petiot, at Harry's New York Bar, appears in Harry MacElhone's *Harry's ABC of Mixing Cocktails*:

In shaker or directly in large tumbler: ice, 6 dashes of Worchester Sauce, 3 dashes of Tabasco, pinch of salt, pinch of pepper, juice of ½ lemon, 2 ounces of vodka, fill remainder of glass with top quality tomato juice, and above all no celery salt.

Immediately following Prohibition, millionaire John Astor VI persuaded Pete to move to New York City and become the "Captain of Bars" at the St. Regis Hotel, and bring the Bloody Mary with him. Rumors abound as to the Bloody Mary's namesake. Most ascribe it to "Bloody Mary" Tudor, daughter of Henry VIII, who was known mainly for restoring the Catholic Church to England and burning her enemies ruthlessly at the stake. But some believe it may have been named in honor of Mary Pickford, the cinematic superstar of her time.

By all means try Pete's original Bloody Mary recipe. But for those who desire a more adventurous version, I highly recommend trying the Blond Mary. This drink was created for the "World of Flavors" conference at the Culinary Institute of America in California's Napa Valley. The use of freshly prepared yellow tomato juice makes it over-the-top delicious. A definitive eye-opener, I enjoy it all on its own, as a morning-after pick-me-up, or as a spicy accompaniment to a special brunch.

1 ½ oz (45 ml) chili pepper-infused Finlandia vodka

5 oz (150 ml) fresh yellow tomato juice

½ oz (15 ml) fresh-squeezed lemon juice

Dash balsamic vinegar

2-3 dashes Tabasco green pepper sauce

Pinch ground white peppercorns

Pinch ground cumin

Pinch sea salt

Pinch paprika

Fresh basil sprigs

Add the above ingredients to an ice-filled mixing glass, saving the basil and paprika until last. Roll until blended. Strain into an ice-filled goblet. Garnish with basil sprig and paprika.

BLUEGRASS COBBLER

Whiskey is a grouchy old bachelor that stubbornly insists on maintaining its own independence and is seldom found in the marrying mood.

DAVID A. EMBURY, *THE FINE ART OF MIXING DRINKS*

A major highlight of each year's Kentucky Bourbon Festival is the Master Distiller's Auction, where devotees watch with envy as little pieces of bourbon history and legend—various bottles of rare and prized product—are offered on the block. The Bluegrass Cobbler originally featured one of these gems: Elmer T. Lee Single Barrel, named for the venerated master distiller himself. Revised for consumption on a wider scale, the current recipe calls for another of Elmer's award-winning bourbons: Blanton's, the first-ever single-barrel bourbon.

While attending the Master Distiller's Auction one year, there was a bottle of Elmer T. Lee Single Barrel on offer, signed by Elmer himself. With a final bid of $80.00, I recall hearing, "...going once, going twice...Sold!" at the very moment I was shooting an enthusiastic wave of greeting across the room to Julian Van Winkle, another of bourbon's elite. The next thing I heard was, "Sold to the highest bidder for $85.00...Thank you, Mr. Abou-Ganim!" The honest truth, and a fortuitous blunder.

The Bluegrass Cobbler celebrates this most excellent American spirit and one of its most talented masters in a style of drink preparation dating back as far as bourbon itself.

2 oz (60 ml) Blanton's Single Barrel bourbon

½ oz (15 ml) Luxardo Maraschino liqueur

2 oz (60 ml) fresh lemon sour

2 pineapple sticks (without skin)

4 Bing cherries, pitted

2 orange slices

In a mixing glass, muddle 1 orange slice, 1 pineapple stick, and 3 Bing cherries. Add bourbon, Maraschino liqueur, and fresh lemon sour. Shake with ice until well blended. Double strain into a crushed-ice-filled Old Fashioned glass. Garnish with remaining fruits.

BRASS RAIL COCKTAIL

To me, the bar after dinner is the final act of the evening and the bartender is one of the lead performers on this dimly lit stage.

SALVATORE CALABRESE, *CLASSIC AFTER-DINNER DRINKS*

Volumes have been written about the "after-dinner drink" and its special place within spirits culture, yet there is no strict or universal consensus as to which drinks qualify. There are countless from which to choose, ranging from the classic *digestivo*, such as armagnac, brandy, port, cognac, and whiskey, to the exotic and highly complex plant liqueurs like Bénédictine and Chartreuse, which were originally produced as medicinal "restoratives." As London-based mixologist Salvatore Calabrese stresses, regardless of whether you choose port, cognac, liqueur, or grappa, "what matters is that you drink something strong, full of flavor, and with an exciting finish." I believe after-dinner drinks are made so by those who enjoy their ritual...partaking of a flavorful libation to cap off the culinary part of the evening, and to raise the curtain for the next act.

The Brass Rail Cocktail includes B&B, or Bénédictine and brandy. The monks of the Bénédictine Abbey of Fécamp, France, developed Bénédictine in 1510. It was originally intended as a restorative or medicinal potion and remains among the oldest surviving liqueurs available today. Its secret recipe of 27 herb, spice, and fruit ingredients is, to this day, both unchanged and highly guarded. Here I've paired it with a premium rum, Cruzan Single Barrel. The Cruzan Distillery in St. Croix produces a single barrel made from a blend of rums, aged up to 12 years, with a second aging in a single, new American cask. It is buttery and full-bodied with hints from the tropics—banana, mango, and ginger.

The Brass Rail Cocktail was inspired by my cousin Helen's penchant for a nightcap to close out the evening after a special occasion; her particular favorite was a B&B. Of course, in those days, that meant producing a Pousse Café glass of Bénédictine to which a careful float of brandy was added. Correct presentation meant layering, a basic bartending task that was one of the first I delighted in mastering.

1 ½ oz (45 ml) Cruzan Single Barrel rum

¾ oz (22.5 ml) B&B

1 ½ oz (45 ml) fresh lemon sour

1 tsp (5 ml) egg white

2 dashes Angostura orange bitters

In a mixing glass, add rum, B&B, fresh lemon sour, egg white, and orange bitters; shake with ice until well blended. Strain into a chilled cocktail coupe. Garnish with the essence of a burnt orange twist, and discard. Sprinkle surface with ground cinnamon.

"When done correctly, a burst of flame will come from the oils being released out of the orange peel."

CABLE CAR

...flexibility and a genial attitude of experimentation are distinguishing marks of the expert beverage chemist. Recipes are as necessary as the traveler's maps, but they are never immutable. To violate a favorite recipe wisely may be to produce a new and superior concoction.

"G. A. C.," *The Art of Mixing Drinks*, 1938

The Cable Car is a simple balance of Captain Morgan spiced rum, orange curaçao, and fresh lemon sour, served up in a cinnamon-sugar rimmed cocktail glass. Perhaps the best known of my original recipes, it was created in 1996 as a signature cocktail for Harry Denton's Starlight Room, a nightclub and cocktail lounge atop the historic Sir Francis Drake Hotel in San Francisco. One of the city's landmark properties, the Sir Francis Drake is located along the world famous Nob Hill cable car tracks. Its Starlight Room is affectionately referred to as the lounge that can be found "between the stars and the cable cars."

Founded in 1983, Captain Morgan is the top-selling spiced rum in the world. Produced by the Serralles Distillery in Ponce, Puerto Rico, it's lush with flavors of nutmeg, clove, cinnamon, and vanilla. A slightly bitter complement, orange curaçao works nicely with the spicy sweetness of the rum. Curaçao, a generic reference to orange liqueur, is so named for an island in the Dutch West Indies where some of the finest bitter oranges in the Caribbean are cultivated. The peels of these unique citrus fruits were brought to Holland in the seventeenth century, where the first orange liqueur was created. Today, this versatile liqueur is primarily produced in France, Holland, and the United States, and still features the aforementioned Caribbean peels.

It has been some time since I left beautiful San Francisco, but this wonderful tipple lives on—rich, smooth, and delicately spicy.

1 ½ oz (45 ml) Captain Morgan Spiced rum

¾ oz (22.5 ml) Marie Brizard orange curaçao

1 ½ oz (45 ml) fresh lemon sour

In a mixing glass, add spiced rum, orange curacao and fresh lemon sour; shake with ice until well blended. Strain into a chilled cinnamon-sugar rimmed cocktail glass and garnish with an orange spiral. To sugar-cinnamon rim a cocktail glass, first chill the glass, then rub the rim's circumference with a lemon wedge. Dip the rim into a bowl with a mixture containing 1 teaspoon (5 ml) ground cinnamon and ½ cup (120 ml) superfine sugar (regular granulated sugar does not adhere as well).

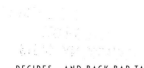

CHAMPAGNE CELEBRATION

He who never takes risks never gets to drink champagne.

RUSSIAN PROVERB

The term "toast" may have come from the Roman custom of placing a piece of burnt bread into a goblet of wine, to improve its flavor before the vessel would have been passed around and shared by all. Several sources indicate that one of the earliest recorded toasts took place during a great feast in 450 A.D., given by the British King Vortigen as he wished for the good heath and fortune of his guests. Today, the champagne-based cocktail has become popular for celebrating important occasions, whether an intimate party for two or a gathering of grand proportions.

Bubbly purists may cry sacrilege at the use of champagne in a cocktail, but there is no arguing with the numbers. According to Jared Brown and Anistatia Miller in their book, *Champagne Cocktails*, it is estimated that in France alone, one out of five bottles of champagne find their way into cocktails. There is nothing sexier than a champagne cocktail. All the senses are invoked: the color, aroma, and flavor of citrus against cognac and champagne; the flow of tiny bubbles rising to the surface; the music of fine crystal flutes meeting one another. The Champagne Celebration is an elegant drink at the top it its class—a celebration in a glass!

I suggest serving the Champagne Celebration as a really simple way to amplify the festiveness of your next soiree, be it for two or two hundred. Your toast, of course will depend on the occasion, but my favorite standby hearkens back to King Vortigen's original... "To good health, good fortune, and infinite happiness!"

1 white raw-sugar cube saturated with Peychaud's bitters

½ oz (15 ml) Rémy Martin VSOP cognac

½ oz (15 ml) Cointreau

Chilled champagne

In a crystal champagne flute, place a bitters-saturated white raw-sugar cube. Next add cognac and Cointreau; slowly fill with ice-cold champagne. Garnish with an orange spiral. (It is best to chill the Rémy Martin and the Cointreau by placing them in the refrigerator before use).

CHERRY CAIPIRINHA

The greatest accomplishment of a bartender lies in his ability to exactly suit his customer. This is done by inquiring what kind of drink the customer desires, and how he wishes it prepared.

Harry Johnson, *New and Improved Illustrated Bartender's Manual*

The Caipirinha, until recently little known in the U.S., is the national drink of Brazil. This version—like all Caipirinhas—is made with cachaca. Brazil alone boasts some 5,000 different brands of cachaca. This drink's use of Pitu is a wonderful first step into this spirit category. A short time after rolling out a traditional Caipirinha at the Starlight Room in San Francisco, I received a call from Pitu's Martin Friedland, thanking us for using his cachaca. How often does that happen? Today, cachaca has become a legitimate spirit category in the United States, with new industrial and artisanal brands becoming available. But for me, it was Martin Friedland's unwavering passion for cachaca and support for the bartending community that bolstered my affection for this spirit.

The Cherry Caipirinha is a twist on the classic, which is made from combining cachaca and white sugar with muddled lime. One way to introduce the newcomer's palate into the world of Caipirinhas is to include a sweeter fruit along with the traditional lime. This is one of the few drinks where the ice used for preparation remains and is served with the drink—this maintains as much of the fruit essence as possible while providing an extra measure of dilution.

This great warm weather libation takes advantage of one of summer's most amazing flavors. Naturally I recommend reserving this version for when the best cherries are available. Don't hesitate to experiment with other fresh fruits, though; try red raspberries, apricots, mangoes, or blueberries. Just make sure your fruits are fresh and ripe, and have fun!

2 oz (60 ml) Pitu cachaca

1 oz (30 ml) simple syrup

6-8 pitted ripe cherries

½ lime, cut in quarters

Fill an Old Fashioned glass with cracked ice to chill. In a mixing glass, add lime quarters, simple syrup, and cherries. Muddle to extract juice without forcing the rind from the lime. Dump the ice from the Old Fashioned glass into the mixing glass; add cachaca and shake. Pour the entire drink into the now-chilled Old Fashioned glass. Add more ice if needed and serve with a swizzle stick.

CHOCOLATE NUDGE

The coldest winter I ever spent was a summer in San Francisco.

MARK TWAIN

Although the term "Nudge" does not delineate a specific style of drink, many will recognize the Coffee Nudge, so popular in the bars and cafes of San Francisco's glorious North Beach neighborhood. Locals are all too well acquainted with the often bone-chilling effects of the coastal fog. Seeking shelter to consume adult beverages of the warm and cozy variety is a beloved custom. The Coffee Nudge is made up of Kahlúa, brandy, and dark crème de cacao mixed with freshly brewed coffee—the hotter the better—topped with hand-whipped cream. The Chocolate Nudge, rather than being coffee based, relies on homemade hot chocolate for its steamy warmth. As for the balance, Kahlua—with its tones of coffee, vanilla, and herbs—connects perfectly with amaretto's soothing almond base.

Amaretto is another liqueur with an ancient lineage. The secret family recipe of the Italian house of Disaronno was created in 1525 as a gift to Bernardino Luini from a beautiful young lady innkeeper who fell passionately in love with him. As a token of her affection she created this sweet, almond-flavored liqueur.

There is still nothing more satisfying to ward off those winter chills than a steaming cup of hot chocolate. So here's the adult version, which comes with considerably more kick than that served up in my youth.

16 oz (480 ml) whole milk
8 tablespoons (120 ml) Ghirardelli sweet ground chocolate
2 oz (60 ml) Kahlúa
2 oz (60 ml) Disaronno Originale amaretto
Freshly whipped cream

In a saucepan, gradually heat milk, adding chocolate and stirring until steaming. Pour into two large, heated coffee mugs. Add equal parts Kahlúa and amaretto to each, and top with fresh whipped cream. Garnish with ground chocolate. Serves two—it's more fun to drink this with a friend!

CLERMONT SMASH

The respectable amount of bourbon to pour in a glass is about two fingers worth. Lucky for me I have big fingers.

Booker Noe

In his legendary book, *The Fine Art of Mixing Drinks*, David Embury describes the Smash of old as a large drink of crushed ice, flavored with mint leaves and a "spirituous liquor," garnished with a selection of fruits. The original Mint Julep is a fine example of an early Smash, minus the fruity decoration. Somewhere along the line the Smash and Julep parted company, with the Smash losing its stature...literally; in contemporary mixology, the Smash is actually a short drink of crushed ice and a base spirit flavored with fresh muddled mint and sugar.

The Clermont Smash is a twist on the classic with a decidedly southern flair. Clermont, Kentucky is where Jacob Beam first distilled his whiskey in 1795, where Jim Beam established his distillery after Prohibition's repeal, and where seventh-generation Master Distiller Fred Noe continues to produce award-winning whiskey today. Knob Creek, named for Abraham Lincoln's childhood home, is full bodied and richly textured, with notes of caramel, vanilla, and dried fruits.

Aside from the use of stellar bourbon, the secret to the Clermont Smash is really three-fold. First, the use of freshly picked spearmint leaves for muddling and garnish; second, the use of falernum syrup in place of sugar; and third, the use of Fee Brothers peach bitters in place of the traditional. Peaches and bourbon—two more harmonious companions are hard to find.

I was honored to learn that Fred Noe himself—Jim Beam's great-grandson—is a fan of this drink. When making yours at home, remember this is not a drink to be rushed. The continual stirring not only frosts the glass but also gives the mint and bourbon a chance to get well acquainted.

2 oz (60 ml) Knob Creek bourbon whiskey

¾ oz (22.5 ml) John Taylor's Velvet falernum syrup

10–12 spearmint leaves

3 dashes Fee Brothers peach bitters

2 oz (60 ml) fresh lemon sour

In an Old Fashioned glass, muddle the spearmint leaves with the falernum syrup, then fill the glass with crushed ice. In a mixing glass, add bourbon, fresh lemon sour, and peach bitters; shake with ice until well blended. Strain into your prepared Old Fashioned glass and stir until the glass begins to frost. Rim the lip of the glass with pineapple, and garnish with a pineapple spear and sprig of mint.

CUPID'S FLIP

Praised be the three aims of life, virtue (dharma), prosperity (artha), and love (kama), which are the subject of this work.

Kama Sutra

This drink is all about sharing the love. Chocolate—the most sensual of gastronomic delicacies—has been associated with passion and romance for centuries. The Aztecs believed it would invigorate a man while effectively muting a woman's inhibitions, and Casanova is said to have used it as an aphrodisiac. It turns out they may not have been too far wrong.

Chocolate contains naturally occurring substances reported to lift one's mood, which also are thought to affect the area of the brain responsible for feelings of attraction, bonding, and love.

As the name suggests, Cupid's Flip is a Valentine's Day specialty cocktail. This is one, frankly, that deserves to be its own course—to be consumed just before retiring to the bedroom, perhaps? It is a rich creation that marries chocolate, vanilla, and almond flavors in a creamy base.

Since Valentine's Day comes but once a year, I suggest you try mixing up a few of these when you next hope to light the proverbial fires.

1 oz (30 ml) Baileys Irish Cream

1 oz (30 ml) Disaronno Originale amaretto

1 oz (30 ml) Bols Crème de Cacao White

½ oz (15 ml) heavy cream

Splash of grenadine syrup

In a mixing glass, add Irish cream, amaretto, crème de cacao, heavy cream, and grenadine syrup; shake with ice until well blended. Strain into a chilled cocktail glass. Garnish with shavings of bittersweet chocolate.

DON FACUNDO

Daisies and Fixes...bear in mind...are drinks of the Mid-Victorian Era. Put on your hoop skirt and bustle or wax your mustache, and sip them to the dreamy rhythm of a Viennese waltz.

DAVID A. EMBURY

This drink reflects a style of preparation similar to the "Fix," which is distinguished by the use of pineapple syrup along with lemon juice, sugar, and a base spirit. Long before there existed the landslide of cocktail modifiers, accents, exotic fruit juices, purées, liqueurs, and mixes we have today, cocktail syrups held center stage. These tend to be concentrated and, like all flavoring agents, should be used in the smallest of doses to prevent their flavor from obliterating all others.

The Don Facundo was created to pay homage to Don Facundo Bacardi, founder of the Bacardi distillery in Santiago de Cuba, circa 1862. Cuba was traditionally considered to produce the finest rum in the world (though today, of course, rums of exceptional quality are produced all around the Caribbean). Cuba was the birthplace to some wonderful cocktails, many presumably containing Don Facundo's rum—the Daiquiri perhaps most celebrated of all.

The Don Facundo takes the Fix to the next level—it's a drink I'm very proud of as an example of an updated classic.

2 oz (60 ml) Bacardi 8 rum

¾ oz (22.5) Marie Brizard orange curaçao

¼ oz (7.5 ml) Fee Brothers pineapple syrup

2 oz (60 ml) fresh lemon sour

2 pineapple spears, one with skin removed for muddling, and one with the skin intact for garnish

In a mixing glass, add skinless pineapple spear and muddle it with the pineapple syrup. Add rum, orange curacao, and fresh lemon sour. Shake with ice until well blended. Strain into a cracked-ice-filled Old Fashioned glass. Garnish with remaining pineapple spear and swizzle stick.

EASY LIVING

Eating, drinking, and carrying on.

ADELAIDE BRENNEN

This drink recipe is a modern twist on the classic combination of rum, sugar and lime juice—the "island trinity" used in Caribbean drinks such as the Daiquiri, Swizzle, Mojito, and the somewhat lesser-known Ti Punch.

At its foundation, this short drink houses Rhum Clément VSOP from the island of Martinque. In 1887, Homère Clément, known as the father of Rhum Agricole, purchased the sugar plantation Domaine de l'Acajou and began producing rhum. Clément VSOP is aged in French and American oak, and yields flavors of vanilla, caramel, coconut, and banana, accompanied by hints of various spices and dried fruits.

In this era of increased attention to premium spirits in general, I'm encouraged to see new interest paid to liqueurs. These have infinite flavor pairing possibilities, and should never be overlooked when it comes to thinking up new drinks. Domaine de Canton, used here, is produced in Jarnac, France, using eau de vie, VSOP & XO Grande Champagne cognac, and Vietnamese baby ginger, adding up to a uniquely lovely liqueur.

I first had the pleasure of serving the Easy Living at Tales of The Cocktail, the annual gathering of bartenders, spirit experts, enthusiasts, writers, producers, and all-around cocktail geeks held every July in New Orleans. (And believe me, July in New Orleans can bring on some kind of thirst.) This particular year, I was pairing cocktails with the wonderful food of Ti Martin & Lally Brennan at Café Adelaide, which is also home to the Swizzle Stick Lounge. Not only did I come to love this drink, but I also discovered a new appreciation for Rhum Agricole.

1 ½ oz (45 ml) Rhum Clément VSOP

¾ oz (22.5 ml) Domaine de Canton ginger liqueur

2 oz (60 ml) pineapple juice

1 oz (30 ml) fresh-squeezed lime juice

In a mixing glass, add rhum, Domaine de Canton, pineapple juice, and hand-extracted lime juice; shake with ice until well blended. Strain into an ice-filled Old Fashioned glass. Garnish with two thin slices of lime.

"A hand-held lime squeezer is invaluable for extracting fresh lime juice at the moment you are preparing a drink."

FRESH FRUIT BELLINI

[When asked what makes a great bar] *"The key word is familiarity, creating a mood, an ambiance, whereby the customer feels he has been invited as a special guest in your own home. You must listen to the client like a friend, the service must be perfect, the decor, the barman. And of course, there is the smile. There must always be the smile."*

CLAUDIO PONZIO, HARRY'S BAR

The Bellini was created in the 1940s at Harry's Bar in Venice, Italy by proprietor Giuseppe Cipriani. The rose-colored paintings of Giovanni Bellini, reflected in the drink's hue, are believed to be the inspiration for its name. This is a very simple drink to make, consisting of only two ingredients—fresh white peach purée and prosecco, an Italian sparkling wine. The difficulty lies in the extremely brief season enjoyed by white peaches.

A story: one year while I was attending the Aspen Food & Wine Classic, Mario Batali invited me to demonstrate the making of Bellinis during one of his cooking seminars. Afterwards, he asked if I ever made Bellinis with fruits other than white peaches. Being a bit of a traditionalist, I answered that for me, the Bellini is a distinctive drink made only of fresh white peach purée and prosecco, and is not a style of drink, such as a Sour or Fizz, with which you could experiment. He disagreed—and I was given pause. True, the classic Bellini is spectacular, and made more so by its fleeting presence. However, eventually I let down my traditionalist guard.

As with many of my other drink recipes, I thoroughly enjoy making and sampling various incarnations of this drink as the seasons change. All, of course, are inspired by the simple, perfect original. To get you started, these four recipes are perhaps my favorite thus far.

CLASSIC (WHITE PEACH) BELLINI

2 oz (60 ml) fresh white peach purée

3 oz (90 ml) prosecco sparkling wine

Simple syrup (quantity determined as below)

1. Select very ripe white peaches.

2. Blanch peaches in boiling water for approximately 1 minute, then transfer them to an ice bath.

3. Peel the peaches and remove their stones.

4. In a food processor, purée the peaches with simple syrup (approximately 1 oz (30 ml) per pound (0.5 kg) of fruit). Hint: Add a couple of red raspberries for color.

5. Sample. Sweeten to taste if needed with more simple syrup.

6. In a mixing glass, add ice, 2 oz (60 ml) chilled purée, and 3 oz (90 ml) chilled prosecco, then roll the drink between the mixing glass and a mixing tin to blend.

7. Strain into a chilled champagne flute.

(CONTINUED ON NEXT PAGE)

FRESH FRUIT BELLINI (CONTINUED FROM PREVIOUS PAGE)

STRAWBERRY BELLINI	BLACK & BLUE BELLINI	APRICOT BELLINI
2 oz (60 ml) fresh strawberry purée	2 oz (60 ml) fresh blackberry & blueberry purée	2 oz (60 ml) fresh apricot purée
3 oz (90 ml) prosecco sparkling wine	3 oz (90 ml) prosecco sparkling wine	3 oz (90 ml) prosecco sparkling wine
Grand Marnier (quantity determined as below)	Simple syrup (quantity determined as below)	Simple syrup (quantity determined as below)

STRAWBERRY BELLINI

1. Select ripe, red strawberries.

2. Rinse, hull, and slice the berries.

3. In a large glass bowl, dust the strawberries with superfine sugar and Grand Marnier (Approximately ½ cup [120 ml] per quart of berries). Cover and refrigerate overnight.

4. Transfer the marinated strawberries to a food processor and purée.

5. Strain through a course sieve to remove the seeds.

6. In a mixing glass, add ice, 2 oz (60 ml) of chilled purée, and 3 oz (90 ml) of chilled prosecco, then roll the drink between the mixing glass and a mixing tin to blend.

7. Strain into a chilled champagne flute.

BLACK & BLUE BELLINI

1. Select 1 pint (480 ml) each of fresh blackberries and blueberries.

2. Purée the berries in a food processor, adding simple syrup to taste.

3. Sample. Sweeten to taste if needed with more simple syrup.

4. Strain purée through a course sieve to remove blueberry skins and blackberry seeds.

5. In a mixing glass, add ice, 2 oz (60 ml) chilled purée, and 3 oz (90 ml) chilled prosecco, then roll the drink between the mixing glass and the mixing tin to blend.

6. Strain into a chilled champagne flute.

APRICOT BELLINI

1. Select very ripe apricots.

2. Blanch apricots in boiling water for approximately 1 minute and then transfer them to an ice bath.

3. Peel the apricots and remove their stones.

4. Transfer peeled apricots to a food processor adding simple syrup to sweeten.

5. Sample. Sweeten to taste if needed with more simple syrup.

6. In a mixing glass, add ice, 2 oz (60 ml) chilled purée and 3 oz (90 ml) chilled prosecco, then roll the drink between the mixing glass and a mixing tin to blend.

7. Strain into a chilled champagne flute.

FRIA CAFÉ ITALIANO

The only way to get rid of a temptation is to yield to it.

OSCAR WILDE

This after-dinner cocktail is so delectable it easily stands as a dessert course on its own. The incomparable triad of vanilla, chocolate, and espresso is the key to the Fria's success. There is of course every opportunity for such a mixture to become cloying and overpowering. The secret, as always, is finding the exact balance between ingredients, and then adding that little something more.

The Molinari family in Civitavecchia, Italy originally developed Sambuca Molinari in 1945. It is a sweet, strong liqueur formulated through a process of steam-distilling star anise seeds. There are other manufacturers of sambuca. Molinari, however, is the only one designated "extra" by the Italian Courts—a classification that may only be worn by products maintaining an extraordinarily high level of quality and consistency.

This drink was born from the desire to develop an after-dinner cocktail with a decidedly Italian tone—it could be considered my answer to the Espresso Martini. Not quite ready to call it a night after finishing your evening meal? Let the evening linger just a little longer over a duet of Frias.

1 oz (30 ml) Navan vanilla cognac
1 oz (30 ml) Godiva chocolate liqueur
1 oz (30 ml) chilled espresso
1 oz (30 ml) heavy cream
Splash Molinari sambuca

In a mixing glass, add Navan, chocolate liqueur, espresso, heavy cream, and sambuca; shake with ice until well blended. Strain into a chilled cocktail coupe. Garnish with ground espresso.

FUNKY MONKEY

It must be done with love. You learn the measurements, but you need not measure—use your feel, your personality! The touch is born in your heart. Any job you do with love is an art. Remember, it is not a frozen drink! It is not a sorbet! Creamy, creamy!

RICARDO GRACIA

Mount Gay Eclipse comes from beautiful Barbados, and is produced by the oldest rum distillery in the world. I consider this a complex rum, its distinct layers enhanced through oak aging—vanilla, cocoa, and caramel as well as fruity notes of prune, mango, and banana that bestow a tropical character. By adding a few flavor companions to this complex rum—banana, crème de banana, and dark crème de cacao—you can uncover a unique alternative to the Piña Colada.

Mention a tropical flavored, poolside refreshment and usually a blended drink comes to mind—Daiquiris, Piña Coladas, and the like. This blended delight is one of the few Abou-Ganim originals made using a blender, which in this case is a necessity for incorporating the fresh banana evenly throughout.

Skill in using a blender can be a wonderful asset, but it is by no means a requirement when mixing drinks. More often than not, blending a drink when you are using only fresh, natural juices will dilute its flavor and diminish the final product. The key when blending is to use a high-quality machine, and practice, practice, practice, in order to keep the flavor balance intact. This is as good a drink to practice with as any. Fans of the Funky Monkey claim it to be both refreshing and restorative—perhaps thanks to the potassium-rich bananas?

This is the perfect summertime beverage for those who like a tropical drink with a creamy texture, and it's a great complement for spicy foods. Thinking of a luau? Cut the tops off some coconuts and serve your Funky Monkeys island style!

1 oz (30 ml) Mount Gay Eclipse rum

¾ oz (22.5 ml) Bols Crème de Bananes

¾ oz (22.5 ml) Bols Crème de Cacao Brown

3 oz (90 ml) homemade coconut milk (page 76)

1 small ripe banana

In a blender can, add rum, crème de banana, crème de cacao, coconut milk, and banana. Add 2 cups (480 ml) cracked ice and blend until creamy. Pour into an empty coconut shell or a goblet. Garnish with toasted coconut. Serve with straws. Reminder: always add the liquid ingredients to your blender first. Hint: if you use the really ripe bananas nobody wants, you will get the best flavor.

GEORGE

The first glass is for medicinal purposes, the second glass makes you happy, and with the third you eat the wind.

A TRADITIONAL AXIOM ABOUT ARAK

Arak—also referred to as arrak, arrack, or raki—is a word of Arabic origin, meaning any distilled spirit. What we call arak today is distilled from grapes, grain, dates, and sugarcane (or palm sap) and flavored with anise seed. El Massaya arak is produced in Lebanon from special varieties of sweet mountain grapes and natural anise seed. Bottled at 100 proof, the essential oils produced through distillation are soluble in high-proof alcohol, yet insoluble in water—this is why good arak will turn milky white and release its floral bouquet when water is added. Back in the seventeenth century, arak was used as the base spirit in many punch recipes brought from India to England.

My introduction to arak came at a very tender age (observational only, of course). My father kept his precious bottle of the stuff tucked in the kitchen cabinet next to Mom's baking pans—it was clear, bearing no label. To a young child it looked like water, but anyone who has ever tasted it unwittingly would never make that mistake twice. It was only brought out for very special occasions. On those occasions, I would beg my father to do the "magic trick." This entailed pouring a few ounces of arak into a double Old Fashioned glass, adding ice, and then adding water. Magically, the clear liquid would turn milky white. I was always so impressed.

Keeping my father's tradition alive, I too keep a bottle of arak at home. And in his honor I developed George, a wonderful, refreshing short drink that can be served as an apéritif with a nice selection of *mazza* (small plates of food such as hummus and grape leaves). I also like to serve arak as an after-dinner drink with a little ice and water, a magic potion with an eternally special place in my heart.

1 oz (30 ml) El Massaya arak
1 oz (30 ml) Plymouth gin
Dash Fee Brothers rhubarb bitters
½ oz (15 ml) fresh-squeezed lime juice
2 oz (60 ml) pineapple juice

In a mixing glass, add arak, gin, bitters, lime juice, and pineapple juice. Shake with ice until well blended. Strain into an ice-filled Old Fashioned glass. Garnish with a skewer of pineapple chunks.

GOLDEN DRAGON

I have taken more out of alcohol than alcohol has taken out of me.

WINSTON CHURCHILL

The Golden Dragon features coconut milk—a wonderful yet often misused modifier. This is not the canned coconut milk you purchase at the grocers, which is really more of a coconut water (though by the way that does go great with fresh lime juice, sugar, bitters, and rum, à la Ernest Hemingway), but a coconut milk made from scratch. In this drink I pair it with Bacardi 8, a unique rum allowed to mature in small oak barrels, where it eventually mellows into a rich, beautifully balanced spirit with flavors of coconut, orange, molasses, vanilla, clove, and almond. Behind the more prominent elements of coconut and rum, this drink is balanced with sweet vermouth and the rarely utilized orgeat.

The simple act of rinsing the glass with sweet vermouth brings a freshness to an otherwise flavor-packed creation. At first taste—and not from a straw, or the whole effect will be missed—the sweet, sensuous highlights of luscious grapes and citrus greet the tongue before the coconut's richness takes over. Orgeat is a sweet, nonalcoholic almond syrup that also happens to be one of the most-often overlooked ingredients in Trader Vic's famous Mai Tai. A light dusting of ground cinnamon finishes the Golden Dragon beautifully.

This is the perfect drink to serve after a long day at the beach, sitting out on the patio watching the day pass slowly into night. It offers the rare quality of being both refreshing and, to a certain extent, restorative.

1 ½ oz (45 ml) Bacardi 8 rum

½ oz (15 ml) Martini and Rossi sweet vermouth

½ oz (15 ml) orgeat syrup

3 oz (90 ml) homemade coconut milk (page 76)

Chilled soda water

Ground cinnamon to sprinkle

Coat a Collins glass with sweet vermouth. Discard excess and add ice. In a mixing glass, add rum, orgeat, and coconut milk, then shake with ice until well blended. Strain into seasoned Collins glass and spritz with chilled soda water. Garnish with a light dusting of ground cinnamon. Hint: the best way to "spritz" a drink is to strain the contents of your mixing tin into the prepared glass as you add small amounts of soda water.

HARD EIGHT

Ran into a chum with a bottle of rum and we wound up drinkin all night.

JIMMY BUFFET

It can be a real challenge to decide the perfect name for a new drink, even though inspiration is all around. It makes perfect sense to consider a drink's city of origin, for example. There may be inspiration from the ingredients, or from the colors revealed as one spirit plays off another in the glass. There are drinks named to honor the time of day, season of the year, holiday or special occasion, and famous people or events. Then there are names that emerge on a whim and work great, "just because"…and the Hard Eight is one of them. It was created in Las Vegas, where gambling delights so many, so why not borrow a little of its vernacular? Those of you who have spent time at a craps table, or suffered a misspent youth shooting dice after school, will recognize a Hard Eight as a pair of fours.

Haitian-based Barbancourt produces what is known as "rhum agricole"—rhum derived from sugar cane juice rather than molasses. Their complex eight-year-old rhum, referred to as Five Star or Réserve Spéciale, gains even further depth of flavor with the aid of time. Aged in French Limousin oak, it's flavored with broad strokes of vanilla, honey, nuts, and cocoa. This is a fine spirit that can be enjoyed on its own, of course, but with the right balance of ingredients its beauty will not be lost, as you will see with this very sophisticated long drink.

This is the perfect beverage to enjoy while shooting craps and a great complement to a fine cigar.

2 oz (60 ml) Rhum Barbancourt Five Star

½ oz (15 ml) fresh-squeezed lime juice

2 dashes Peychaud's bitters

Chilled ginger beer

Build in an ice-filled Collins glass, adding rhum, lime juice and bitters. Top with ginger beer and stir. Garnish with a sprig of mint.

HOT BUTTERED RUM

Cocktail is a stimulating liquor, composed of spirits of any kind, sugar, water and bitters. It is vulgarly called a bittered sling and is supposed to be an excellent electioneering potion, in as much as it renders the heart stout and bold, at the same time that it fuddles the head...

THE BALANCE AND COLOMBIAN REPOSITORY, 1806.

Hot Buttered Rum dates as far back as George Washington's time, when the drink was a handy and persuasive political tool to warm hearts and open minds to the "message" at hand. That said, clearly it is great for larger parties and holiday celebrations since the batter stores well and can be made in quantity ahead of time. Personally, I prefer its effect on gatherings of much smaller scale. Use this recipe for any gathering filled with holiday cheer; it's been known to make the toes tingle and the heart merry.

This interpretation features Mount Gay Extra Old rum—a perfect match for the drink's rich buttery batter. In truth, any of the great aged rums on the market would also serve. Just be sure to look for one that is complex, with lots of character. For a change, try using one of the spiced rums.

This has always been one of my holiday favorites—a delightful way to warm the bones when the weather turns frosty. Be sure to make a little extra batter—it will package nicely in an airtight container, and it makes a great holiday gift, along with a special bottle of rum of course!

TONY'S HOT BUTTERED RUM BATTER

1 lb (454 gm) light brown sugar

½ lb (227 gm) unsalted butter (softened)

2 teaspoons (10 ml) ground cinnamon

2 teaspoons (10 ml) ground nutmeg

½ teaspoon (2.5 ml) ground allspice

2 teaspoons (10 ml) pure vanilla extract

FOR EACH DRINK

1 ½ oz (45 ml) Mount Gay Extra Old rum

Boiling water

In a mixing bowl, beat together softened butter, brown sugar, vanilla, and spices until well combined. Refrigerate in an airtight reusable container—it is best to make the batter at least 48 hours in advance of using, so the spices have an opportunity to mingle (it will store for up to a month). Be sure to remove the batter from the refrigerator at least 6 hours prior to serving, to allow it to soften.

In a preheated coffee mug, combine 2 heaping tablespoons of batter with the rum. Top with 6 oz (180 ml) of boiling water and stir well to mix. Serve with a spoon.

JAMAICAN SUNSET

Anybody who says I didn't create this drink is a dirty stinker.

TRADER VIC, REFERRING TO OTHERS'
CLAIMS ON HIS MAI TAI RECIPE

This drink pays homage to the illustrious Mai Tai, one of the most popular and least understood of the classics. The Mai Tai was created in 1944 by Victor Bergeron, a.k.a. "Trader Vic," as an original creation served at his restaurant in Oakland, California. His recipe of Jamaican rum, orange curaçao, orgeat, rock candy syrup, and fresh lime juice has been fiddled with more than most, and poor Vic was so bothered by this that he felt the need to set the record straight in 1972, when he revised his *Bartenders Guide,* by asserting that the drink is his and his alone, despite claims to the contrary.

Order a Mai Tai and, depending where you order it, there is no telling what you will be served. The Jamaican Sunset is not a Mai Tai, but a direct descendent of what might be called one of the many "Mai Tai mishaps." In this case, creative license yielded agreeable results. It is a spiced-up version of what frequently masquerades as Vic's creation, but strictly speaking it is not, nor does it claim to be, an improvement on the original—merely an evolutionary relation.

Aside from abiding by the cardinal rule of using only fresh-squeezed juices, it's the combination of Sailor Jerry Spiced rum in concert with the conspicuously rich Myers's Jamaican dark rum that brings complexity and balance to this drink. Myers's is one of the truly legendary names in the rum world. It has been produced by Fred L. Myers & Sons, at the Moneymusk Distillery in Jamaica, since 1879.

The Jamaican Sunset is one of my poolside favorites. When the mood calls for a rich, flavorful, fruity rum-based cooler, give this one a go. And if your travels bring you within reach of one of his namesake restaurants, by all means stop in and give Trader Vic and his delectable Mai Tai a nod.

| 1 ½ oz (45 ml) Sailor Jerry Spiced rum |
| 1 ½ oz (45 ml) fresh-squeezed orange juice |
| 1 ½ oz (45 ml) pineapple juice |
| 1 oz (30 ml) fresh lemon sour |
| ½ oz (15 ml) Myers's Original dark rum |
| ¼ oz (7.5 ml) Sonoma Syrup Co. pomegranate syrup |

In a mixing glass, add spiced rum, orange juice, pineapple juice, and fresh lemon sour; shake with ice until well blended. Strain into an ice-filled Collins glass. Add pomegranate syrup and watch it slowly descend to the bottom. Top with a float of dark rum—you'll see how the name came to mind.

JOY RIDE

A great cocktail is about the journey, not the destination.

TONY ABOU-GANIM

The Joy Ride features a sophisticated disposition, the product of its clean, bracing combination of flavors. It's a wonderful way to introduce those who may be a little timid to the world's number-one aperitivo—Campari. This phenomenal product was created in the mid-1800s by Gaspare Campari in Milan, Italy, during an era when fashionable cafes and bars had their own *maitre licoristes*—a "master of drinks" or mixologist of sorts, skilled at formulating recipes from a wine or spirit base, combined with select herbs and spices.

Campari is produced through a process that creates a vibrant, ruby-red elixir with an extremely concentrated flavor profile—one that is neither for the faint of heart nor heavy of hand. This unique aperitivo commands respect from all who approach.

Featured prominently in two famous classic cocktails, the Americano and the Negroni, the complexity and power of Campari simply aches for a citrus companion. And, as it's only a delicate 24 percent alcohol by volume, it works as a wonderful modifier against a higher-proof spirit. The clean lines of Ketel One's Citroen works very well on both fronts. Unlike many citrus vodkas that use a blend of fruits, Citroen is produced primarily using lemons, leaving it forward enough for Campari's depth and complexity.

Just prior to moving to Las Vegas, I performed in a play called *Joy Ride* with a wonderful San Francisco theatre group called Campo Santo. This cocktail was named for the experience. Of course the play is now just a fond memory, but the drink lives on in dedication to its cast and crew.

1 ½ oz (45 ml) Ketel One Citroen vodka

¾ oz (22.5 ml) Campari

3 oz (90 ml) fresh lemon sour

1 teaspoon (5 ml) egg white

Chilled soda water

In a mixing glass, add vodka, Campari, fresh lemon sour, and egg white; shake with ice until well blended. Strain into an ice-filled goblet and spritz with chilled soda water. Garnish with 3 lemon slices fanned.

"To make fresh lemon sour, simply mix two parts fresh, filtered (to remove the pulp and seeds) lemon juice with one part simple syrup."

JUST FOR MARY

The cocktail hour is still an enchanting experiment in time. It can transform a life, launch a career, or ignite a romance in a matter of minutes.

JOSEPH LANZA, *THE COCKTAIL*

The cocktail hour will always possess a certain "something" that sits just beyond definition. The "hour," being a collective state of mind rather than a position on the clock, is that wonderful time of day when we gather, reflect on the day's triumphs or tragedies, and enjoy a favorite libation before heading home or venturing out, transformed, for the evening and delights to come. For me, the cocktail hour will always inspire and captivate for its sense of mystery, intrigue, and the allure of what lies beyond.

Inspired by the Manhattan—a classic and rather serious cocktail-hour libation—and by the qualities expressed in my dear friend and writing partner, the Just for Mary emerged with ease. Mary is one of the most enigmatic people I know. She has expressive brown eyes. They penetrate, but do not reveal. She often speaks with an economy of words, yet relays several layers of intent. She can be surprised but never startled. When approached, she retreats, evaluates, and then decides. If she is pleased, you may see a Mona Lisa smile—just lingering a moment. What lies beyond? In this case, an occasion for a truly civilized if not enigmatic cocktail—one with a straightforward, quiet beauty, and a decidedly sophisticated presence.

(ri)1 straight rye whiskey (pronounced "rye one") is made for mixing. Light among its rye brethren, pleasing, with both fruit and spice flavors at its center, it is tantalizing, friendly, and "easy on the tongue." I combined (ri)1 with Lillet Blond and presented it to Mary. She smiled but I could tell something was missing. Back to the liquor cabinet for a measure of Cherry Heering and some orange bitters, then finished with burnt orange twist essence and a brandied cherry. This time a *big* smile. It may have been "just for Mary," but thankfully there was enough for two. I think you'll agree that this is a perfect cocktail-hour elixir.

2 oz (60 ml) (ri)1 straight rye whiskey
½ oz (15 ml) Cherry Heering
½ oz (15 ml) Lillet Blond
2 dashes Regan's Orange Bitters No. 6

In an ice-filled mixing glass, add rye whiskey, Cherry Heering, Lillet, and orange bitters. Stir until very cold. Strain into a chilled cocktail glass. Finish with the essence of a burnt orange twist and discard. Garnish with a brandied cherry.

LEMON ORCHID

It's never too early for a cocktail.

NOEL COWARD

To call the Lemon Orchid a "lemonade" is somewhat misleading. It has a wonderful blend of tropical flavors, made up of Aperol, Alizé Gold passion fruit liqueur, and of course homemade lemonade. This is a unique apéritif-style drink, in that it does not rely on a high-proof spirit as its base. The result? A light and playful cooler.

The final recipe—themed around passion fruit, both tropical and exotic—eventually solidified after I appraised a generous selection of liqueur and fruit flavor combinations (a necessary exercise considered to be one of mixology's professional perks). Alizé Gold is a unique combination of aged cognac and a blend of select varieties of exotic passion fruits, including the most prevalent tropical species—the *Passiflora Edulis Forma Flavicarpa*, with its exotic spicy flavor. At just 16 percent alcohol by volume, it is infinitely mixable and lends itself rather nicely as a lemonade partner. The rhubarb and orange notes of the Aperol work to complete this drink's fruity balance.

When you are looking for a thirst quencher that is both light in alcohol and clean against the palate, this is the ticket. I like to enjoy this drink when something really light is what suits. Great for a brunch or earlier afternoon gathering.

1 oz (30 ml) Alizé Gold passion fruit liqueur

1 oz (30 ml) Aperol

The flesh of one whole passion fruit

4 oz (120 ml) homemade lemonade

Slice your passion fruit down the middle and scoop the pulpy center with a spoon directly into a mixing glass. Add Alizé, Aperol, and fresh lemonade. Shake with ice until well blended. Pour entire contents of your shaker into a goblet. Add additional ice if needed. The seeds of the passion fruit are edible, included in this drink to serve as its garnish.

LLOYD'S SWIZZLE

Dedicated to the incomparable Lloyd, R.I.P., for years of creative inspiration, enduring strength, and unwavering loyalty ... in that four-legged, distinctly bulldog sort of way.

The Swizzle, a style of drink that originated in the West Indies, was traditionally prepared with the aid of a tropical bush. An authentic cocktail swizzle, as it happens, is the branch of said bush, with three to five small forked branches at its terminus. Once placed into a glass or pitcher primed with ingredients, the stem would be firmly pressed between the palms, and the branch, or "swizzle," would be twirled back and forth. When swizzled rapidly enough, the drink was mixed quite effectively, to the point of foaming and frothing its contents as well as producing a cooling frost on the outside of the glass.

The first known rum Swizzle recipe has been credited to the Georgetown Club in British Guiana, and contains the delightful combination of rum, simple syrup, lime juice, bitters and crushed ice. Lloyd's Swizzle is a close cousin to the Georgetown Club original, with the addition of the apricot hue introduced via Rothman & Winters apricot liqueur—a great complement to the rich fruit flavors of a hearty rum. Although not strictly required by definition, if a drink is classified as a Swizzle, it most likely contains rum. I make Lloyd's Swizzle with Appleton Estate V/X rum—full-bodied, pot-distilled, and oak-aged, it's rich and complex with ripe apricot, orange, and vanilla. Most importantly, of course, this is prepared using a cocktail swizzle and good old-fashioned elbow grease.

You will certainly impress your guests if you perfect the art of swizzling. Remember, in order to make a really authentic Swizzle, it will be necessary to track down a really authentic cocktail swizzle. A traditional wooden swizzle is a unique tool to own, but the modern version—which resembles a hand mixer's beater with a longer handle—is my preference. In a pinch, a long-handled spoon with holes or slots in the bowl will suffice.

1 ½ oz (45 ml) Appleton Estate V/X rum

½ oz (15 ml) Rothman & Winter Orchard apricot liqueur

1 oz (30 ml) simple syrup

1 oz (30 ml) fresh-squeezed lime juice

2 dashes Angostura bitters

Fill a Collins glass three-quarters full with crushed ice, then add rum, apricot liqueur, simple syrup, lime juice, and bitters. Place the swizzle into the glass and, using the palms of your hands, swizzle away. Add additional crushed ice and continue swizzling until the drink is thoroughly mixed and the glass frosts. Garnish with a sprig of mint.

LUCE DEL SOLE

Don't worry about a thing, every little thing is gonna be alright.

BOB MARLEY

The Luce del Sole was inspired by my first encounter with Finlandia's Grapefruit vodka, which happened while I was attending the Midnight Sun Celebration held each year in Lapland, Finland. Bartenders from around the globe came to shake cocktails, unite with fellow mixologists, eat reindeer sausage, partake of the mandatory sauna, and of course to celebrate the longest day of the year, when the sun never sets. Needless to say it was some party!

Being a bit of a Campari fanatic, and conscious of needing to employ alternatives, I was thrilled when Aperitivo Aperol became available in the United States—and I no longer had to smuggle it back two bottles at a time on my rare trips to Italy. Created in 1919 by the Barbieri brothers, Aperol is a classic aperitivo and a great match for Finlandia's honest grapefruit tones. Only 11 percent alcohol and featuring flavors of bitter orange, rhubarb, and gentian, Aperol can be enjoyed alone over ice, or in a classic Spritz, or of course in a cocktail such as the Luce del Sole!

I had the great privilege of traveling the country and part of the world with Dale DeGroff, conducting vodka tastings and bartender trainings on behalf of Finlandia (the program was affectionately known as Finnishing School). After 3 years we had visited 42 markets in 6 countries, and the Luce del Sole was one of the many drinks delivered in those seminars.

1 ½ oz (45 ml) Finlandia Grapefruit vodka

¾ oz (22.5 ml) Aperitivo Aperol

½ oz (15 ml) honey syrup

1 oz (30 ml) fresh-squeezed lemon juice

1 oz (30 ml) fresh-squeezed orange juice

In a mixing glass, add vodka, Aperol, honey syrup, and lemon and orange juices; shake with ice until well blended. Strain into an ice filled Old Fashioned glass. Garnish with an orange spiral and lemon slices.

LYCHEE SAKE MARTINI

Sakenomi jozu wa nagaiki jozu, "To know how to drink properly is to know longevity"

For mixologists, the realm of "flavored Martinis" is a slippery slope at best. So often, things that were once classic, refined, and revered are later embraced with such enthusiasm that, through the process of celebrating the thing, we manage instead to transform it right out of recognition. The trick is not to obscure the presence of the "Martini" under all that "flavor." Accordingly, the Lychee Sake Martini adheres to what should be the flavored Martini mantra: subtlety and balance above all else.

A good-quality sake's delicate flavor requires a careful hand when it comes to cocktail pairings. Lychee fruit has fragrant, subtly sweet meat, somewhat similar in consistency to that of a grape. First cultivated some 2,000 years ago in the Fukien and Kwangtung provinces of southern China, the lychee became the pride of many imperial households as a symbol of romance and love—the perfect yang to sake's ying. Include just the right measure of Chopin potato vodka, with its creamy mouth feel and hint of toffee sweetness, and the Lychee Sake Martini is born. Subtlety and balance above all else.

This is one of the few instances where a canned fruit performs better than its fresh counterpart. Consider making your next sushi meal a take-out, or try making your own at home and distinguish the occasion with a Lychee Sake Martini or two. Save room for the lychee fruit garnish. It makes for the perfect finish to your meal.

1 ½ oz (45 ml) Chopin vodka

1 oz (30 ml) lychee syrup (syrup that comes with canned lychees)

2 oz (60 ml) Kurosawa Junmai Kimoto sake

In a mixing glass, add vodka, sake, and lychee syrup; shake with ice until well blended. Strain into a chilled cocktail coupe. Garnish with a speared lychee fruit.

MARGARITA PRIMO

The origin of a cocktail can be, as we shall see, a difficult fact to establish.

COLIN PETER FIELD, *THE COCKTAILS OF THE RITZ PARIS*

The Margarita's genesis has been the source of much speculation. Woven within and among countless theories rest certain claims that most industry experts feel sure of—or more accurately, *almost* sure of. First, the Margarita was created somewhere between the mid 1930s and late 1940s. Second, it hails from either Mexico or California…or possibly Texas or New Mexico. It would simply take too long to recount all the claims for where and how this fabulously popular drink was invented.

The Margarita is one of the most consumed drinks in the United States. If there was ever a recipe that demanded the use of top-quality ingredients, this is the one. This Margarita is made "primo" through the use of one of the ultimate silver or blanco 100 percent agave tequilas on the market, plus Cointreau and the use of freshly extracted juices. Forget the dreaded burning fumes and head-pounding aftermath that went with the inferior products of your past. True 100 percent agave tequilas are so pleasing and smooth, they are in fact as superb for sipping solo as they are in a Margarita—definitely no salt or lime are needed in either case.

Although this drink originally featured Herradura Silver 100 percent agave tequila, there are so many amazing options out there that I really hesitate to suggest one brand in particular. Further, while the mixology elite would nearly always characterize the Margarita as requiring silver or blanco tequila, some days just require a little something different. I am not at all opposed to mixing up a Margarita with one of the aged tequilas, either a reposado or añejo. Are the aged tequilas more appropriate for sipping than for use in a mixed drink? Perhaps, but the additional complexity of flavor in the aged tequilas bring plenty to this classic drink.

2 oz (60 ml) 100 percent agave silver tequila

1 oz (30 ml) Cointreau

2 oz (60 ml) fresh lemon sour

1 oz (30 ml) fresh-squeezed lime juice

In a mixing glass, add tequila, Cointreau, fresh lemon sour, and lime juice; shake with ice until well blended. Strain into an ice-filled goblet. Garnish with a wedge of lime. I do not advocate salting the glass, but if you must, simply moisten the rim with fresh lime juice, then dip lightly into a plate of kosher salt.

MOM'S SANGRIA

Don't drink to get drunk. Drink to enjoy life.

JACK KEROUAC

Introduced to the United States during the 1964 World's Fair in New York, Sangria is a favorite among mixologists, amateur and professional alike. Originally from Spain, this red wine punch is likely derived from Sangaree—a potent mixture popular in the 1800s, fashioned from wine, port, sherry, beer, liquor, or Madeira, along with sugar, ice, and fresh fruit, and finished with a dusting of nutmeg. From its humble beginnings, Sangria has matured into the quintessential Spanish party drink enjoyed the world over.

Sangria's building blocks generally include red wine, fresh fruit, fruit juices, brandy, and soda. There is no limit—aside from imagination—as to the style of Sangria one can create. What's more, rarely will two batches of the same recipe yield quite the same drink. A few more common variations involve a substitution for the red wine base. Sangria Blanco, for example, is made with white wine. Do you prefer sparkling wine, or rosé? As long as the rest of the ingredients are complementary, why not? As for pairing, if grilled Cuban dry-rubbed pork tenderloin is on the menu, a classic big Spanish red wine Sangria is ideal. For marinated grilled gulf prawns, think about a Pinot Grigio and fresh pear Sangria. Go ahead and get creative!

My mother was a wonderful cook and loved to entertain. Her culinary repertoire was full of authentic Lebanese dishes in deference to my father's native cuisine. She discovered that Sangria was a perfect match for many family meals. The next time you entertain with a Mediterranean tilt, or serve up a batch of juicy grilled hamburgers, this may be your beverage of choice. Remember, it tastes infinitely better if you prepare it a day in advance, allowing time for the ingredients to mingle.

BATCH RECIPE—SERVES 15

2 bottles of Spanish Rioja, 25 oz (750 ml) each
12 oz (360 ml) Hennessy VS cognac
12 oz (360 ml) Cointreau
6 oz (180 ml) simple syrup
12 oz (360 ml) fresh-squeezed orange juice
12 oz (360 ml) fresh-squeezed lemon juice
2 cinnamon sticks
3-4 lemons, cut into thin quarters
20 strawberries, sliced
3-4 small oranges, cut into thin quarters
Chilled lemon-lime soda

Place all of the above ingredients (except the lemon-lime soda) into a large glass container. Cover and refrigerate overnight. When ready to serve, pour into an ice-filled pitcher until two-thirds full. Add freshly sliced fruits and top with lemon-lime soda. Stir gently to mix. Serve with fresh fruit in an ice-filled goblet.

MY MARTINI

This is the violet hour, the hour of hush and wonder, when the affections glow again and valor is reborn, when the shadows deepen magically along the edge of the forest and we believe that, if we watch carefully, at any moment we may see the unicorn. But it would not be a martini if we should see him.

BERNARD DEVOTO, *THE HOUR*

My personal journey with the perfect Dry Martini has been a winding one. I passionately agree with William Grimes's assertion in his *Straight Up or On The Rocks* that the Martini is "the quintessential cocktail, the standard by which all others are judged." The perfect Dry Martini is among the most disputed cocktails: shaken vs. stirred, gin vs. vodka, olive vs. twist, how much vermouth vs. not at all.

Admittedly, what was once my perfect Martini has in fact evolved. Originally committed to shaken and only shaken, I have now moved my preference to gracefully stirred, and I now prefer considerably more French dry vermouth than I once did. In *The Hour*, DeVoto maintains, "There is a point where the marriage of gin and vermouth is consummated. It varies a little with the constituents, but for a gin of 95 proof and a harmonious vermouth it may be generalized as about 3.7 to 1." This is a perfect proportion in my opinion. When ordering I do suggest, however, you consider rounding off to a ratio of 4 to 1; requesting fractions from a bartender may seem a shade arrogant.

It is impossible to say which gin is ideal—this is a highly personal decision. I recommend you experiment to see what you enjoy most. My choice tends to be driven by my particular mood at the given moment: sometimes a big, robust, juniper-forward gin is ideal, but at times a softer, floral, fruity or feminine gin can be just right. Good fortune for us all that there are so many varieties to choose from, each creating its own special memory in the end.

¾ oz (22.5 ml) Noilly Prat dry vermouth
2 ½ oz (75 ml) gin of choice
1 large Spanish olive, stuffed with Maytag Blue cheese

Fill a mixing glass with large cube ice. Add vermouth and gin. Stir until ice-cold, as my cousin Helen said, "20 times to the right and 20 times to the left." Strain into a chilled cocktail glass. Garnish with a single Maytag Blue-stuffed olive.

NEIGHBORHOOD NEGRONI

I like to say that we are in the 't' business...Integrity, Loyalty, Creativity, Credibility.

Fritz Maytag, Anchor Brewery & Distillery

The Negroni is one of the most sophisticated of classic cocktails, and it may prove to be an acquired taste for many cocktail novices. It was created in the early 1920s by Count Camillo Negroni, who along with a bartender named Fosco Scarselli, was said to have developed the recipe at Casoni, a café on Florence's famous Via Tomabouni. The Count ordered it with such frequency that eventually the drink and the Count became synonymous.

What then makes a Neighborhood Negroni? It is blessed with the presence of the exquisite Junipero gin, produced by the Anchor Distilling Company located in the Potrero Hill neighborhood of San Francisco. According to Fritz Maytag, Junipero is bottled at 98.6 proof and flavored with more than a dozen botanicals, including orange and lemon peel, juniper berries, caraway, coriander, anise, fennel, and ginger, to name a few. This is one of the classics that can be built over ice as a short drink—as it would be served when ordered in Italy—although I prefer mine served up, as a cocktail.

Of course you can make a Negroni with any premium gin, and your choice will bring its own unique flavor to the cocktail. But to make the Neighborhood Negroni remember Fritz's Junipero gin. And don't forget the burnt orange garnish.

1 oz (30 ml) Junipero gin

1 oz (30 ml) Campari

1 oz (30 ml) Martini and Rossi sweet vermouth

In an ice-filled mixing glass, add gin, Campari, and sweet vermouth; stir until well chilled. Strain into a chilled cocktail glass. Garnish with a burnt orange twist. For the Italian version, build the drink in an ice-filled Old Fashioned glass by adding gin, Campari, and sweet vermouth. Stir and garnish with an orange slice.

(CONTINUED ON PAGE 150)

NEIGHBORHOOD NEGRONI

(CONTINUED FROM PAGE 148)

"You will want to stir any drink that is made up of spirit only—for example, a Negroni or Manhattan. Stirring a cocktail requires the use of the mixing glass portion of a Boston shaker set and a long-handled barspoon.... How long is best to stir? I stand by Helen David's advice: 'Stir 20 times to the right and 20 times to the left.'"

PASSION PUNCH

Enjoy a pisco libation and free the Latin lover in yourself.

Diego Loret De Mola

A Punch can be fashioned as an individual drink—such as the Planter's Punch—or as a batch mix served from a bowl. Introduced to the U.S. from the East Indies by way of the English, the word "Punch" is actually derived from the Hindi word "panch," or "five." The earliest recipes were composed of five ingredients: a distilled spirit—originally arak, then eventually rum; water or tea; spice; lemon or lime juice; and sugar. With the passage of time, Punch evolved into any drink made with rum, brandy, whiskey, gin, vodka, or other spirits, mixed with fruit juice, sugar, soda, spice and water (or ice).

Fans of Vic Bergeron, a.k.a. Trader Vic, and Donn Beach, a.k.a. Don the Beachcomber, will recognize that producing an exquisite punch of the single-serving variety involves real proficiency behind the bar—the party bowl variety being much more forgiving in terms of preparation. The Passion Punch is a direct attempt to mimic the "solo-Punch" of old, distinguished by its carefully balanced combination of spirits working in harmony with a variety of tropical fresh fruits and juices. The foundation for this recipe comes from Barsol pisco. Pisco is a brandy made from several different grape varieties and is produced in either aromatic or nonaromatic varieties. Barsol Quebranta is made from nonaromatic grapes, yielding fruity, floral notes of fresh grape and peppery spice. Mixed with the full-bodied Myers's rum from Jamaica, the Barsol pisco combines to provide a harmonious platform for this very tropical treat.

Pisco is a spirit that's starting to get more and more recognition. Two of the best-known pisco drinks are the Pisco Sour and the Pisco Punch, but let's not stop there—take a cue from the Passion Punch and try fashioning your own pisco creation.

1 ½ oz (45 ml) Barsol Quebranta pisco

½ oz (15 ml) Myers's rum

1 oz (30 ml) passion fruit purée

2 oz (60 ml) fresh-squeezed orange juice

2 oz (60 ml) fresh lemon sour

2 dashes Angostura orange bitters

A pinch of freshly grated nutmeg

In a mixing glass, add pisco, passion fruit purée, orange juice, fresh lemon sour, orange bitters, and grated nutmeg; shake with ice until well blended. Strain into an ice-filled goblet. Top with a float of Myers's rum. Garnish with orange and lemon slices and a Maraschino cherry.

PINK FLAMINGO

The principal business of life is to enjoy it.

SAMUEL BUTLER

I have always admired my sister-in-law Janet's flair for generating fun. She and my brother, Dave, still live in our hometown of Port Huron, Michigan, some 50 miles northeast of Detroit along Lake Huron. Midwest natives can attest that their winters are no walk in the park. By late March, everyone is praying for sunshine to replace the snow and rain. Naturally, once summer rolls around, the urge to make the most of it takes over. At first sign of warm weather, the outdoor party season begins.

Among Janet's close group of friends, there is a tradition of taking turns hosting cocktail parties. To avoid wasting precious time organizing by phone, they invented a unique way to let everyone know where the evening's festivities will be held: the hosts du jour place a plastic pink flamingo in their yard—wherever the pink flamingo is displayed, the party is on! Everyone then knows where to head after a long day at the beach with the kids, no questions asked. Janet needed a drink she could serve Punch-style whenever the party migrates to her house, so I created this drink for her.

Besides being a perfectly delicious and refreshing summery cooler, this drink has the added advantage of allowing the hosts to mix a batch in advance, for serving from pitchers. There is no point in having the life of the party stuck in the kitchen when she's needed elsewhere!

1 ½ oz (45 ml) Absolut Citron vodka

½ oz (15 ml) Luxardo Maraschino liqueur

1 ½ oz (45 ml) fresh lemon sour

1 ½ oz (45 ml) white grape juice

1 oz (30 ml) Pom Wonderful pomegranate juice

In a mixing glass, add vodka, Maraschino liqueur, fresh lemon sour, pomegranate juice, and white grape juice; shake with ice until well blended. Strain into an ice-filled goblet. Garnish with lemon slices and sliced green and red seedless grapes.

BATCH RECIPE—SERVES 12-15

33 oz (1 liter) bottle of Absolut Citron vodka

6 oz (180 ml) Luxardo Maraschino liqueur

32 oz (1 liter) fresh lemon sour

32 oz (1 liter) white grape juice

20 oz (600 ml) Pom Wonderful pomegranate juice

Sliced red and green grapes

Mix ingredients in advance, refrigerate until ready. Transfer to an ice-filled pitcher, add lemon slices and sliced red and green grapes, and serve at will.

POMME & CIRCUMSTANCE

Good apple pies are a considerable part of our domestic happiness.

JANE AUSTEN

This apple-on-apple beverage is one I really enjoy, partly for its lineage but also for its rich volume of flavors. Applejack is America's oldest native distilled spirit. William Laird, a distiller who emigrated from Scotland in 1698, is credited with its unique recipe. His son, Robert, served under George Washington in the Revolutionary War, and went on to open Laird and Company in 1780. More than two centuries later, the distillery is still run by Lairds—Larrie Laird and his daughter, Lisa Laird-Dunn. They represent the oldest family of distillers in America.

Laird's Applejack is made from tree-ripened apples grown in the Shenandoah Valley: Jonathans, Winesaps, Stamens, Pippens, and Delicious. The apples are picked at peak harvest—September through November—and pressed into pure juice. This sweet apple "nectar" is allowed to ferment naturally, converting its sugar into alcohol and yielding a hard cider. The cider is then distilled and aged in oak barrels to produce apple brandy. Applejack is a very unique product in that it is not a straight apple brandy, but a blend of apple brandy and neutral spirits. This makes it softer and more compatible for mixing.

This recipe was inspired by my Michigan childhood. We would take trips to the orchard to pick apples, some of which would find their way into one of my Aunt Dort's home-made pies. A warm slice of pie accompanied by a Vernor's ginger-ale float was my particular favorite, a reward for our labor in the orchard. It is the combination of all these flavors (in a fortified sort of way) that led to the creation of the Pomme & Circumstance.

2 oz (60 ml) Laird's Applejack
1 oz (30 ml) fresh-squeezed lemon juice
1 oz (30 ml) ginger syrup
2 oz (60 ml) cloudy, unfiltered apple juice
Chilled Vernor's ginger ale

In a mixing glass, add Laird's, fresh lemon juice, ginger syrup, and cloudy apple juice; shake with ice until well blended. Strain into an ice-filled goblet and top with chilled ginger ale. Stir to mix and garnish with a fan of apple slices.

PUMPKIN NOG

Christmas is not properly observed unless you brew nog for all comers; everybody calls on everybody else; and each call is celebrated by a solemn egg-nogging...

An English visitor in 1866

Egg nog, the rich, spicy alcoholic beverage used to toast one's health, is believed to have found its way into the American holiday tradition by way of Europe, but the source of its name was never concretely identified. The British of old enjoyed a hot beverage made of eggs and milk curdled with the addition of hot ale or wine, called Posset. Taverns would have served their spicy brew in a small wooden mug called a "noggin." Once in Colonial America, rum, also known as "grog," was both popular and plentiful, thus becoming the basic egg nog recipe's spirit of choice. Now, an egg drink mixed with grog...from there, it's not too far to get to "egg nog." Variations of this hearty drink have found their way into many different cultures, each with its own interpretation. There is the Mexican Rompope, Peruvian Biblia con Pisco, Puerto Rican Coquito, and German Biersuppe, to name a few.

The Pumpkin Nog is yet another offspring of the traditional drink: a tasty, spirit-based egg nog with a seasonal twist. This recipe calls on the fresh peach and orange notes of Southern Comfort, which work well with the deep flavors of this nog.

Although egg nog is associated with the holidays, this is a great drink to mix up and share with your loved ones whenever cooler weather moves the party indoors.

BATCH RECIPE—SERVES 15

1 fifth (750 ml) Southern Comfort

12 jumbo eggs

6 cups (1.5 liters) whole milk

½ lb (227 gm) superfine sugar

1 teaspoon (5 ml) pure vanilla extract

1 teaspoon (5 ml) ground cinnamon

½ cup (120 ml) cup pumpkin purée (page 73)

Separate eggs and place egg whites in the refrigerator. In a mixing bowl, beat the yolks until creamy. Gradually add half of the sugar, beating at high speed until thick. Stir in milk, Southern Comfort, vanilla, cinnamon, and pumpkin purée. Place in refrigerator to chill, at least 2 hours. Remove egg whites from the refrigerator and beat until soft peaks form. Add remaining ¼ lb of sugar, beating into stiff peaks. Fold sugared egg whites into the chilled Southern Comfort mixture. Serve in punch cups, and garnish with freshly grated nutmeg. It is fine to substitute canned pumpkin purée if you don't have the time to make your own.

PURE JOY

Today is a beautiful day, don't spoil it by worrying about tomorrow.

Janet Abou-Ganim

According to Dale DeGroff in his book *The Craft of The Cocktail*, the origin of the Fizz as "a spin-off of the Sour" can be traced back to the mid- to late-nineteenth century, when carbonated or "charged" water first became available behind the bar. The great "Professor" Jerry Thomas lists several Fizz recipes in the 1887 revised version of his *Bartender Guide*. Previously, bartenders had made sporadic use of European mineral water, for those who could afford to pay the price. Otherwise, making a fizzy cocktail at home involved using bicarbonate of soda—not an ideal option.

The name Fizz apparently came from the sound created by the release of bubbles as the drink was topped off from a siphon bottle. Some contend that a Fizz should be shaken and strained into a Fizz or Delmonico glass without ice, then topped with seltzer water. Others strain the drink into an ice-filled Highball glass, then spritz with seltzer water. One rule stands firm: the Fizz is served naked, or garnish free.

This drink features one of the most exquisite fruit-spirit combinations, that of gin and raspberry. It is at once seductive and refreshing, making it an ideal summertime cooler. I like to make this drink with Bombay Sapphire, which is lighter in gin's base botanicals (juniper berries and coriander) and presents a more floral, fruity character, featuring botanicals such as orris (the root of the iris flower), lemon peel, and bitter almonds.

I really enjoy creating drinks to honor friends, family, and special occasions. Pure Joy was developed as a special gift to celebrate my niece, Kaitlin Joy, in honor of her graduation. Originally made with Absolut Citron vodka, we switched the recipe significantly to feature Bombay Sapphire after she tried her first perfect Dry Martini.

1 ½ oz (45 ml) Bombay Sapphire gin
½ oz (15 ml) Bonny Doon Framboise
2 oz (60 ml) fresh lemon sour
1 teaspoon (5 ml) egg white
4-5 red raspberries
Chilled seltzer water

In a mixing glass, muddle red raspberries and framboise. Add Bombay Sapphire, egg white, and fresh lemon sour; shake with ice until well blended. Double strain into a Fizz glass and spritz with chilled seltzer water.

PURGATORIO

*Drink and be merry, for our time on earth is short,
and death lasts forever.*

A MPHIS (330 BC)

One of the most intense events in my career was competing on Food Network's *Iron Chef America*, pairing drinks alongside Mario Batali's culinary offerings in "Battle Mango." It was a supercharged hour spent sweating, mixing, listening to the clock tick down, sweating some more, and frantically working in the now while thinking ten steps ahead. One minute everything was smooth sailing, and the next, I had a cut finger and somehow managed to freeze up the ice cream maker! It was a walk—well, maybe more of a race—through the culinary version of purgatory, and somehow I survived.

When mango was revealed as the secret ingredient, Belvedere Orange immediately came to mind—orange and mango being a really flavorful match. Moroccan and Spanish fruit peels are macerated in Belvedere spirit, releasing their natural flavors before being redistilled in copper alembic pot stills.

This cocktail also calls upon a unique modifier, St. Germain elderflower liqueur. This is a delightful and intriguingly versatile liqueur made from fresh elderflower blossoms. The fresh elderflower infusion is blended with eau de vie (grape spirit) and sweetened with pure cane syrup to produce an artisanal floral liqueur, with additional notes of pear, grapefruit, and lychee. Those interested in reaching beyond the basics should consider placing this in their repertoire.

A unique experience beyond compare—and one of the most exciting yet stressful hours of my life! Battle Mango pitted Mario and myself against challengers Chef Robert Gadsby and Mixologist (and dear friend) Bridget Albert. I am pleased to say that though it was truly a competition, it was an entirely friendly one.

1 ½ oz (45 ml) Belvedere Orange vodka

½ oz (15 ml) Aperitivo Aperol

½ oz (15 ml) St. Germain elderflower liqueur

1 oz (30 ml) fresh mango purée

½ oz (15 ml) fresh-squeezed lime juice

In a mixing glass, add vodka, Aperol, St. Germain, mango purée, and lime juice; shake with ice until well blended. Strain into a chilled cocktail coupe. Garnish with a burnt orange twist.

"Ice is perhaps the single most overlooked ingredient in drinks preparation, yet one of the most important."

SERRANO COCKTAIL

Others have seen what is and asked why. I have seen what could be and asked why not.

PABLO PICASSO

Commissioned by Executive Chef Julian Serrano, this cocktail serves as the signature apéritif for Bellagio's Picasso in Las Vegas. Picasso quickly developed a reputation for offering a fine dining experience as delicious as its space is exquisite. With its cuisine in the masterful hands of James Beard Award-winning Serrano, and the restaurant design executed by Pablo Picasso's son, Claude, the results could only be spectacular.

Julian expressed his desire for a cocktail that would "prepare the palate" for his guests' upcoming meal. Considering his vision for Picasso's cuisine, I wanted a cocktail featuring Campari. To avoid overpowering or negating the unique quality Campari brings to this cocktail, I paired it with an equal amount of limoncello. With a vodka base and fresh-squeezed orange juice for balance, the Serrano Cocktail is a delightful combination of flavors with a vibrant piquancy all its own.

This has become one of my personal favorite apéritif-style cocktails. Taking Campari as an aperitivo is an extremely civilized Italian tradition, though one that has yet to take hold in the United States. Take a chance when planning the next dinner party; include a pre-meal Campari cocktail to entice your guest's palate.

1 ½ oz (45 ml) Skyy vodka

½ oz (15 ml) Campari

½ oz (15 ml) Toschi limoncello

1 ½ oz (45 ml) fresh-squeezed orange juice

In a mixing glass, add vodka, Campari, limoncello and orange juice; shake with ice until well blended. Strain into a chilled cocktail coupe. Garnish with a lime spiral.

SPICED CIDER TODDY

Rock & Rye can be served hot with excellent effect to fight off colds, influenza's, miasmas, megrims, swamp mists, and blackwater fevers. In fact any sort of excuse seems to work.

CHARLES H. BAKER, JR., *THE GENTLEMAN'S COMPANION*

There was a time when most bars had their own recipe for making Rock & Rye, a traditional wintertime elixir that was commonly believed to hold medicinal properties of sweeping proportions. Whether used to ward off sickness or to aid digestion, this creation involved dissolving rock candy in rye whiskey, with the addition of fruit. It would then be served neat, on the rocks or with hot water and a slice of lemon as a Toddy. Its value as a cure-all was not the only key to its success—according to the *Esquire Drink Book*, 1956:

> *Once upon a time, a person afflicted with rasp, or contemplating the possibility that he might be in the near or distant future, would prepare his remedy by putting rock candy and citrus fruit slices and peels into a jug of rye, corking, and setting it aside...The only trouble is that sympathetic friends who rush to the sick one's bedside will want to share his medicine (which has the taste and texture of a liqueur), possibly forgetting to leave a thimbleful for him.*

Rock & Rye is a wonderful thing to keep around the house—to help ease you through those long, cold winter nights. Who knows? It may very well prove a great elixir for weathering one of those pesky colds!

Despite the passing years, I have never lost my love for hot apple cider, although this version isn't for the kids.

BATCH RECIPE—SERVES 15

25 oz (750 ml) homemade Rock & Rye (page 65)

1 gallon (3.8 L) apple cider

½ cup (120 ml) clover honey

5 cinnamon sticks

30 whole cloves

1 vanilla bean, sliced lengthwise

In a large saucepan, combine cider, honey, and spices. Bring to a boil and let cool for at least 4 hours. Remove spices and reheat when ready to serve, adding the Rock & Rye at the last moment. Serve in heated mugs.

ST. PATTY'S COFFEE

Cream as rich as an Irish brogue, coffee as strong as a friendly hand, sugar as sweet as the tongue of a rogue, and whiskey as smooth as the wit of the land.

JOE SHERIDAN, INVENTOR OF THE IRISH COFFEE

March 17, 460 A.D., marks the death of Ireland's beloved patron saint, and was initially observed as a religious feast day known as St. Patrick's Day. The tradition traveled to North America in 1737, when the city of Boston first embraced the custom of public celebrations. The first ever St. Patrick's Day Parade, however, took place not in Boston, nor Ireland, but in New York City, circa 1762.

Fast-forward a few hundred years to contemporary festivities and the old saying "Everybody's Irish on St. Patrick's Day" starts to make sense. The biggest gathering is likely Dublin's St. Patrick's Day Festival—a fusion of religious and secular celebrations attended by nearly 1 million revelers.

Irish whiskey has long battled the stigma of not mixing well in cocktails, which quite frankly is unfounded, for its flavor complexity clearly offers great mixing possibilities. These whiskies stand out from their Scottish neighbors primarily because their barley is not kilned over an open peat fire—hence the lack of smokiness. Jameson Irish whiskey comes from the Midleton Distillery in the beautiful County Cork. Its hints of oak, vanilla, caramel, and baked apple make this 80 proof whiskey ideal for mixing drinks.

This Eire-bent drink is for those of you who, come St Patrick's Day, are up for something other than green beer. Although clearly a drink to consider on March 17, don't be put off by the name. There is no reason it can't be enjoyed year round.

1 oz (30 ml) Jameson Irish whiskey

¾ oz (22.5 ml) Baileys Irish cream

¾ oz (22.5 ml) Nocello walnut liqueur

Fresh brewed coffee

Freshly whipped cream

In a heated Irish coffee glass, add Irish whiskey, Baileys, walnut liqueur, and piping hot coffee. Top with a collar of freshly whipped cream. Garnish with freshly grated nutmeg.

STARLIGHT

The Starlight is a crisp, refreshing cooler that gains much style and sophistication from the brandy that floats atop...

GARY REGAN

The Starlight—notable in part as the first Tony Abou-Ganim original libation, and for being featured in Gary Regan's *New Classic Cocktails*—was created in 1996 as a specialty of the house for the newly remodeled Harry Denton's Starlight Room. Of course, I turned to my old favorite, Campari, and this time paired it with Cointreau, one of the most versatile cocktail modifiers. With a sweet, mildly bitter flavor, strong with the essence of orange peel, Cointreau is a natural Campari complement. The Starlight finds its stride with a float of Germain-Robin—a singular domestic brandy made in the style of a French cognac. Produced in Ukiah, California, it is double-distilled in an alembic still, then aged in French Limousin oak casks. Its distinctive character stems from the use of select California grapes, primarily Pinot Noir, rendering a smooth, harmonious profile unlike anything from France.

Consider making this part of your repertoire of special-occasion drink creations. If your travels take you to San Francisco, stop by the Starlight Room, say hello to Harry, and partake of their namesake drink.

1 oz (30 ml) Campari

1oz (30 ml) Cointreau

1 oz (30 ml) fresh-squeezed orange juice

1 oz (30 ml) fresh lemon sour

Chilled soda water

½ oz (15 ml) of Germain-Robin VSOP brandy

In a mixing glass, add Campari, Cointreau, orange juice, and fresh lemon sour. Shake with ice until well blended. Strain into an ice-filled Collins glass, spritz with chilled soda water, and stir gently. Top with a float of Germain-Robin brandy. Make sure not to serve this with a straw, to enable the drinker to enjoy the brandy floating on top.

SUNSPLASH

A perfect summer day is when the sun is shining, the breeze is blowing, the birds are singing, and the lawn mower is broken.

JAMES DENT

The Sunsplash is a colorful, fun, feel-good sort of drink for a sunny afternoon's gathering with friends. It's a delicious, fruity cooler that doesn't pretend to be anything more than it is—fresh, simple, and delightful. Although originally made with Stolichnaya Ohranj, the recipe lends itself to exploring the many new orange-flavored vodkas that have appeared since I created it. This is a drink recipe that responds favorably to change!

When it comes to flavored vodkas, not all brands are created equal. Flavor can be imparted into vodka in many ways: from dried peels, essential oils, and flower blossoms, all the way down to artificial flavorings (which of course you should avoid at all costs). Solid choices include Belvedere Orange, Absolut Mandarin, Hangar One Mandarin Blossom, Charbay Blood Orange, or Finlandia's Tangerine, to name but a few. One can see how the variations mount. Luckily, any of these are beyond satisfactory—your choice is simply a matter of palate proclivity.

With its vibrant color and delicious balance of fruit flavors, this is just right for your next warm-weather get-together. If you are looking for the perfect "fun in the sun" sort of libation, this should do the trick. By all means, give it a try in its original recipe, or with your own favorite orange vodka.

1 ½ oz (45 ml) Stolichnaya Ohranj vodka
½ oz (15 ml) Cointreau
1 ½ oz (45 ml) fresh-squeezed orange juice
1 ½ oz (45 ml) cranberry juice
1 oz (30 ml) fresh lemon sour

In a mixing glass, add vodka, Cointreau, orange juice, cranberry juice, and fresh lemon sour; shake with ice until well blended. Strain into an ice-filled goblet. Garnish with a slice of orange and a lemon spiral.

TENNESSEE HIGHBALL

Every day we make it, we make it the best we can.

Jack Daniel

This drink ultimately emerged from the search for a superlative way to showcase an exceptional spirit, Tennessee whiskey. The Tennessee Highball is best described as a cross between a Highball and a Sour, with the addition of orange bitters—a largely forgotten ingredient, regarded as a staple behind any well-stocked bar prior to Prohibition. Happily, it is making a comeback.

The famed Jack Daniel's distillery of Lynchburg is recognized as the oldest registered distillery in the United States. Jack himself started producing his whiskey in 1866, and is known to have used the very same recipe of corn, rye, malted barley, yeast, and limestone-rich springwater that his namesake distillery uses today.

While each purveyor's individual recipe, distillation, and aging practice serves to shape a whiskey's character, Tennessee whiskey is different from other American-made whiskeys because it's made with a technique known as the Lincoln County Process—every drop of Tennessee whiskey is mellowed through 10 feet of sugarmaple charcoal.

A number of factors— including warehouse barrel placement, storage temperature, and even the character of a barrel's wood-grain—interact to make a few barrels exceptional in quality terms. Over time the Master Distiller eventually hand-selects barrels containing the absolute pinnacle product, otherwise known as highly coveted "single barrels." This whiskey is sure to yield a memorable cocktail.

2 oz (60 ml) Jack Daniel's Single Barrel Tennessee whiskey

2 oz (60 ml) fresh lemon sour

3 dashes Fee Brothers orange bitters

Chilled dry ginger ale

In a mixing glass, add whiskey, fresh lemon sour, and orange bitters; shake with ice until well blended. Strain into an ice-filled Highball glass, spritz with dry ginger ale, and garnish with freshly cut orange slices and a swizzle stick.

THE CESAR RITZ

Never say no when a client asks for something, even if it is for the moon. You can always try.

CESAR RITZ

The legacy of The Ritz-Carlton begins with the celebrated hotelier Cesar Ritz. His philosophy redefined the luxury hotel experience in Europe through his management of The Ritz Hotels in Paris and London. The history of The Ritz-Carlton Hotel Company, built largely on the legacy of Cesar's efforts, begins with the opening of The Ritz-Carlton, Boston in 1927.

I love the challenge of creating a gin-based cocktail. Plymouth gin is produced at Black Friars Distillery, which was established in 1793, and which is the world's oldest working gin distillery. Their recipe calls for just seven botanicals. It is these, in combination with the use of the coveted local Dartmoor water, that give Plymouth its unique character and taste. The Cesar Ritz calls for the Original Strength, 41.2 percent alcohol by volume, but Plymouth is also available in the Navy Strength, at 57 percent. Plymouth's forward, masculine style provides the necessary support for this recipe's varied flavors.

I had the honor to work with the Ritz-Carlton staff, primarily on reviving the cocktail classics, but also to create a few originals; this one I developed as a signature Martini, calling to mind the timeless elegance of the classic, but featuring a modern flair. I like to think Cesar himself would have enjoyed this.

2 oz (60 ml) Plymouth gin (original strength)

1 oz (30 ml) St-Germain elderflower liqueur

6 chunks of peeled English cucumber

10-12 fresh spearmint leaves

1 oz (30 ml) of fresh-squeezed lime juice

In a mixing glass, muddle cucumber and mint with St-Germain. Add gin and lime juice. Shake with ice until well blended. Double-strain into a chilled cocktail coupe. Garnish with three wafer-thin slices of English cucumber.

THE LAST FRONTIER

The proper drinking of Scotch whisky is more than indulgence; it is a toast to civilization, a tribute to the continuity of culture, a manifesto of man's determination to use the resources of nature to refresh mind and body and enjoy to the full the senses with which he has been endowed.

DAVID DAICHES, *SCOTCH WHISKY*

I created this cocktail as part of a demonstration for a group of journalists on behalf of Chivas Regal Scotch whisky. The event took place in Alaska, at a fishing lodge on Finger Lake. Getting to the lodge required a 50-minute flight aboard a three-seater snow plane out of Anchorage—an incredibly beautiful journey. This was my first opportunity to make cocktails with glacier ice. It was the most amazing ice imaginable, and could potentially have been 8,000 years old.

Chivas Regal is a blended whisky from the Speyside region in the Northeast part of Scotland. Blended Scotch combines several different malt whiskies with lighter, grain whiskies. At the heart of Chivas is Strathisla, a complex Highland malt. Other malts that go into it include Glenlivet, Glen Grant, and Longmorn, to name a few. It is the job of the Master Blender—Colin Scott—to bring them into harmony. While this tipple was created in part to honor the greatly talented Colin, it's also a souvenir of an amazing four-day adventure to one of our planet's remaining unspoiled frontiers.

I realize the possibility of procuring glacier ice is wholly unreasonable—although it does impart a magical quality—I am happy to say high-quality locally produced ice will do.

1 ½ oz (45 ml) Chivas Regal Scotch whisky

½ oz (15 ml) Luxardo Maraschino liqueur

1 oz (30 ml) fresh-squeezed Ruby Red grapefruit juice

1 oz (30ml) fresh lemon sour

Brandied cherries

In a mixing glass, add whisky, Maraschino liqueur, grapefruit juice, and fresh lemon sour. Shake until well blended; strain into a chilled cocktail coupe. Garnish with 2 brandied cherries.

"The key to a great infusion—no surprise—
is to select the freshest, ripest, best ingredients."

TOM & JERRY

In the sweetness of friendship, let there be laughter and sharing of pleasures.

KHALIL GIBRAN

The grandfather of American bartending, "Professor" Jerry Thomas is among those credited with developing the Tom & Jerry—one of the quintessential wintertime drafts. According to his 1862 publication, *The Bar-Tender's Guide or How to Mix All Kinds of Plain and Fancy Drinks*, this seasonal drink was not to be offered until after the first snowfall. For nearly a century, it was a common sight to see a Tom & Jerry bowl in your local watering hole during the holidays. But now this wonderful but labor-intensive drink has all but disappeared. The key to success in making superior Tom & Jerry's is to use fresh batter. You want to be sure each drink is made and served while the batter is still light and fluffy.

Although the classic recipe calls for Jamaican rum and brandy, the potential for spirit and liqueur pairings with this drink are infinite, so don't feel obliged if you want to branch out. This version features Appleton Estate V/X, a full-bodied rum from Jamaica, and Hennessy VS cognac. This is a perfect opportunity to try out your own combination of favorites.

My cousin Helen made Tom & Jerry from scratch for nearly 70 years for her loyal customers at the Brass Rail. Every year on Thanksgiving she unpacked her three commercial mixers and kept them spinning until New Year's Day. I hope you'll agree Helen's recipe is delightful. Her version serves 12... or, as she used to say, "4 friends, 3 mugs each!"

HELEN'S TOM & JERRY BATTER —SERVES 12

8 jumbo eggs

1 ½ (360 gm) cups powdered sugar

½ teaspoon (2.5 gm) cream of tartar

Freshly grated nutmeg

Hot water

Separate egg whites and yolks. In a large mixer, beat yolks until creamy, then transfer them to another bowl. Clean the mixer and add the egg whites and cream of tartar, then beat until stiff. Add powdered sugar and fold in creamed yolks. Mix until batter is light and fluffy.

FOR EACH DRINK

¾ oz (22.5 ml) Appleton Estate V/X Jamaican rum

¾ oz (22.5 ml) Hennessy VS cognac

In a preheated mug, add 2 heaping ladles of batter (roughly 6 oz or 180 ml). Add rum and cognac. Top with hot water and dust with freshly grated nutmeg. Serve with a paddle or spoon.

TONY'S PICK-ME-UP

After any Picker-Upper, let's not lie supine and bewail hard the unjust fate…Any physical activity not including actual death, and no matter how slight or brief, cannot but help.

CHARLES H. BAKER, JR.

Harry Craddock of the Savoy had his. Johnnie Solon of the Waldorf-Astoria also had his. Harry MacElhone of Harry's New York Bar had his. Frank Meier at the Ritz Bar, Paris created one of the most famous, the Corpse Reviver. Charles H. Baker, Jr. dedicates quite a bit of real estate to this category, listing "TWENTY and SEVEN picker-uppers" in his 1939 book, *The Gentleman's Companion*. Many a barman in history has created his own liquid antidote for the dreaded hangover. In keeping with this long-standing tradition, Tony's Pick-Me-Up was designed to help clear the cobwebs lingering from a celebratory "night before." For those looking to ease the suffering just a little, I can tell you this drink—a truly unique mixture of flavor and texture—has been known to help.

Fear not the presence of absinthe in your morning-after restorative. Absinthe, also known as "The Green Fairy," was made illegal in the United States in 1912. Made with anise, fennel, and *Artemisia absenthium*, otherwise known as grande wormwood, it is renowned for its alleged hallucinogenic and addictive properties. Oscar Wilde said about absinthe, "After the first glass, you see things as you wish they were. After the second, you see things as they are not. Finally, you see things as they really are, and that is the most horrible thing in the world." Well, it turned out that the psychoactive properties of absinthe were a little exaggerated. Since 2007 it has once again been legal in the United States. That said, at 120 to 140 proof, use absinthe sparingly!

Whenever friends exhibit signs of their morning-after struggle, I throw together this unique reviver to soften the blow. Contrary to legend, "a little hair of the dog that bit you" really is an old wives' tale. Truth be told, the best remedy for overindulging the night before is time, rehydration, and a bit of sustenance. When feeling the need for a restorative, remember to stay hydrated, get lots of rest, and when the constitution allows, take in a little protein!

1 ½ oz (45 ml) Martel VS cognac
2 dashes Frenet-Branca
2 dashes Lucid absinthe
1 ½ oz (45 ml) fresh lemon sour
1 tablespoon (15 ml) egg white
Ice-cold champagne

Rinse a chilled cocktail coupe with the absinthe, discarding the extra. In a mixing glass, add cognac, Frenet-Branca, fresh lemon sour, and egg white. Shake with ice until well blended. Strain into the absinthe-seasoned cocktail coupe, top with champagne, and drink it, as Harry Craddock once said, "Quickly, while it's laughing at you!"

"You should shake drinks that include any ingredients besides straight spirit."

VANILLA GORILLA

Make a drink, serve a drink. No fieldtrips in between. If you can walk and talk, that's cool, but never leave a cocktail stuck in the pour-mat vortex or your guest will miss the good years of a fine drink.

WILL SIMKINS, A.K.A. VANILLA GORILLA

This after-dinner drink was created to honor a bartender by the name of Will Simkins, known and loved by his friends for, among other things, his reputation as a very big eater. Revered for his ability to demolish a half-gallon of vanilla ice cream—spoon in one hand, bottle of chocolate syrup in the other—and his fondness for enormous meals, he has been dubbed "Vanilla Gorilla" by his fans. Now, whether gorillas are indeed fond of vanilla is "fruit" for another discussion. However, the name Vanilla Gorilla does seem to conjure up visions of lush tropics, where flavors of banana, vanilla, and coconut are a natural fit.

When introducing either vanilla or banana flavors into a drink, there is a danger that either one will overpower everything else. One of the best ways to introduce that hint of vanilla without overpowering the drink is with a vanilla-flavored spirit, in this case Absolut Vanilia. This product features pure natural vanilla—one sip and the taste buds are well on their way to vanilla ice cream.

There are a lot of flavors at work in this recipe. Produced in the Piedmont region of Northern Italy for more than 300 years, Frangelico is an intriguing combination of toasted wild hazelnuts, cocoa, and vanilla flavors. And finally, Lucas Bols—one of the world's oldest producers of liqueurs—makes a crème de banana that is an exquisite balance of chocolate, banana, vanilla, and almond. Each one comes through in this creamy delight.

After-dinner cocktails are one of the nicest and most overlooked customs for ending an evening meal. While it is the perfect complement to a bittersweet chocolate desert, the Vanilla Gorilla can stand confidently alone. By all means, try infusing your own vanilla bean vodka to use in place of purchased—it will be fun to see how yours compares!

1 ½ oz (45 ml) Absolut Vanilia vodka

¾ oz (22.5 ml) Frangelico liqueur

¾ oz (22.5 ml) Bols Crème de Bananes

1 oz (30 ml) heavy cream

First prepare the glass by dipping the rim in chocolate sauce (about ¼ cup poured out on a plate broad enough for the rim of the glass to dip into) and then roll the rim in toasted coconut, (about a ½ cup spread evenly on a flat surface). Chill the glasses in your freezer until ready to serve. In a mixing glass add vodka, Frangelico, crème de bananes, and heavy cream; shake over ice until well blended. Strain into the chilled coconut-rimmed cocktail glass.

VERY SEXY

I had to get a second mortgage to afford the ingredients...

GREG MILLER, ON PREPARING THE VERY SEXY

For this cocktail, I borrowed the term "very sexy" from Grant MacPherson, Bellagio's original executive chef, who would use the phrase to declare an object or creation of utmost perfection: "Those are some very sexy mushrooms," or "His steak frites are very sexy," or, in this case, "That is one very sexy cocktail."

At the heart of this drink lay three main ingredients: a Belvedere Citrus vodka base, a hint of cassis, and a finish of fine champagne. Belvedere is exemplary of Polish-style vodka and thus perfect for use in cocktails, as it maintains a full-bodied character that supports as well as withstands the presence of companion ingredients. The addition of cassis, a liqueur made from black currants, provides an element of fruit without being overly sweet. The finest cassis available is that produced in the Bordeaux and Dijon regions of France—Marie Brizard being among them.

At the finish, nothing is more festive or fitting than a top of champagne to bring a cocktail to life—from the cork's release to the rush of tiny bubbles, this quintessential celebratory libation never fails to infuse that added element of cheer. Needless to say for this drink, only "very sexy" champagnes need apply. One look at the Very Sexy in the glass and all will become clear ... this is one very sexy cocktail.

I was asked by my longtime friend Greg to create a special cocktail to mark the 40th birthday of our dear friend, Pam. Make no mistake, this drink is not for the faint of heart; to this day Greg still comments on the exceptional cost of its compelling ingredients.

1 ½ oz (45 ml) Belvedere Citrus (lemon) vodka

½ oz (15 ml) Marie Brizard Crème de Cassis de Bordeaux

1 ½ oz (45 ml) fresh lemon sour

1 teaspoon (5 ml) egg white

Chilled Moet & Chandon White Star champagne

Grand Marnier

Marinated wild berries

You need to see this drink coming. For best results, 1 pint each of raspberries and blackberries should be marinated in 4 oz of Grand Marnier. Cover and refrigerate for 6 hours. In a mixing glass, add vodka, cassis, fresh lemon sour and egg white. Shake with ice, strain into a chilled cocktail coupe, and add 2-3 each marinated blackberries and raspberries. Top with champagne.

WILD BERRY MOJITO

[The Mojito is] the crowning jewel of any drink card. To master this drink is to tease Zeus himself.

HARRINGTON & MOORHEAD,
COCKTAILS: THE DRINKS BIBLE FOR THE 21ST CENTURY

What the Caipirinha is to Brazil, the Mojito is to Cuba—an inextricable element within Cuban culture, not unlike the island's coveted cigars. Catapulted into the mainstream primarily through the attentions of Ernest Hemingway and his legendary capacity for consuming cocktails, the Mojito is believed to have evolved in the mid-nineteenth century from the Draque, a mixture of rum, sugar, and mint popular with the working man.

The Mojito of today is markedly different from its humble beginnings. Purists will say that it is impossible to make a Mojito that tastes comparable to one constructed in Cuba. Could it be their use of Cuban rum, the native *hierba buena*, or maybe the alluring sound of maracas dancing on the eardrums? No matter: the use of top-quality light rum, fresh lime juice, garden-fresh mint, crushed not cubed ice, and—above all—very careful muddling. Attention to this aspect will yield a delightful Mojito. Musical accompaniment remains optional.

The Wild Berry Mojito is simply a fruity variation of the original. This is a refreshing choice for pairing with anything spicy off the barbeque. Whether enjoying one alone or along with a meal, be sure to relax and savor the experience. As with the original Mojito, this libation actually improves with every sip—as the mint, rum, berries, and lime juice take time to mingle.

1 1/2 oz (45 ml) 10 Cane rum

3–4 each of fresh blackberries, blueberries, and raspberries

12–14 fresh mint leaves

1 oz (30 ml) fresh-squeezed lime juice

1 oz (30 ml) simple syrup

Chilled soda water

In a Collins glass, muddle mint, simple syrup, berries, and lime juice. Fill glass with crushed ice and slowly add rum. Stir well until the ice is reduced by 1/3. Top with more crushed ice, then stir until the glass frosts. Spritz with chilled soda water and stir one last time to incorporate. Garnish with a sprig of fresh mint that has been dusted with powdered sugar and a swizzle stick— this drink benefits from being stirred.

YULETIDE PUNCH

Here's to us all, God bless us every one!

Tiny Tim's toast from *A Christmas Carol*, by Charles Dickens

Serving a Holiday Punch is a most delightful custom, be it celebrating the first snowfall of the season with a couple of Tom & Jerry's, or mixing up a bowl of egg nog to see the family through a long night of Christmas Eve tree trimming. Most countries have their own Holiday Punch traditions. There is Sweden's Glögg, Britain's Wassail Bowl, Germany's Grossmutters Punch, and so on. Each is traditionally served at a gathering of loved ones during the holidays, to accentuate the season's spirit of joy and happiness.

Yuletide Punch is a lighter, fruit-based alternative to the traditional nog, and a little less complicated to prepare. One of the obvious advantages of serving a batch recipe like this one is that most of the recipe can and should be seen to in advance. More than a matter of convenience, allowing the punch to rest allows its ingredients to intermingle, overnight if possible. Final assemblage, however, should take place immediately prior to serving—if possible, just as the first guests are crossing the threshold. This keeps the bubbles from dissipating and the ice mould from overdiluting the recipe before it can be enjoyed. Plus, the host is more likely to get out of the kitchen and join the party.

With a little imagination and pre-party organization, it is possible to make a punch that looks great and tastes even better. A few tips to remember:

- Always use fresh, seasonal fruits and juices
- Always use premium spirits and wines
- Avoid small cube ice, and instead make a large ice mould; this keeps your Punch cold without diluting it and it's easier to maneuver with a serving ladle
- If you're using sparkling wine or carbonated beverages, make sure they are well chilled and wait until the very last minute to add, since the bubbles will soon dissipate
- Be sure to chill your Punch very well in advance, as the ice mould is used to keep the Punch cold, not to chill room-temperature ingredients
- If using fresh berries, always freeze them first to better maintain the look and shape of the fruit

(CONTINUED ON NEXT PAGE)

YULETIDE PUNCH

(CONTINUED FROM PREVIOUS PAGE)

BATCH RECIPE—24 SERVINGS

2 bottles chilled champagne

32 oz (1 liter) Absolut Mandarin vodka

16 oz (500 ml) Marie Brizard Cassis de Bordeaux

32 oz (1 liter) white grape juice

16 oz (500 ml) fresh lemon juice

16 oz (500 ml) fresh-squeezed orange juice

8 oz (240 ml) simple syrup

2 pints blackberries

2 pints raspberries

2–3 oranges, thinly sliced and quartered

2–3 lemons, thinly sliced and quartered

To make fruit ice moulds, I use a Bundt cake pan. The amount of fruit you will need depends on the size of your mould—I generally use 2 pints each of blackberries and raspberries, plus one small navel orange and one lemon cut into wheels. I begin by filling the mould ¼ full of water and adding red raspberries, blackberries, and orange and lemon wheels. I allow it to freeze and add another layer, and so on, until it is full.

Premix the vodka, cassis, white grape juice, fresh lemon juice, fresh orange juice, and simple syrup in a large container, cover, and refrigerate until ready to serve (at least 3 hours, preferably over night). Transfer to a large punch bowl. Add one pint each of frozen blackberries and raspberries, 2 to 3 small oranges and lemons thinly sliced and quartered, fruit ice mould, and chilled champagne just prior to serving. Serve in punch cups.

"Bartenders, home or professional, should own good knives and make sure they're always sharp."

ZIG ZAG

Summer is the time when one sheds one's tensions with one's clothes, and the right kind of day is jeweled balm for the battered spirit. A few of those days and you can become drunk with the belief that all's right with the world.

ADA LOUISE HUXTABLE

This is a crisp, ultra-refreshing cooler developed to feature two of our favorite summertime flavors: lemonade and watermelon. From my childhood, when I'd sit on the back porch with a big wedge of ice-cold melon spitting seeds at my kid brother, to my summer job in Arizona pitching melons with my old friend Nick, I have always been a huge fan of watermelon.

With its bright, clean flavor and naturally sweet juice, watermelon has definitely been underutilized in mixology. Technically classified as a vegetable, this familiar picnic-table side dish is one of nature's perfect snack foods. The *Citrullus lanatus* is made up of more than 90 percent water, and it's a great source of vitamins, potassium, and fiber. Okay, maybe that's not so important within the context of cocktail ingredients, but it's impressive nonetheless.

This one takes a little more preparation than most, but don't be discouraged—it is well worth the effort. Remember, the seedless variety works best for drinks preparation.

1 ½ oz (45 ml) Belvedere Citrus (lemon) vodka

¾ oz (22.5 ml) Cointreau

3 oz (90 ml) fresh-pressed watermelon juice

2 oz (60 ml) fresh homemade lemonade (page 72)

In a mixing glass, add vodka, Cointreau, watermelon juice, and lemonade; shake with ice until well blended, then strain into an ice-filled goblet. Garnish with quarter lemon slices and blueberries.

BATCH MIX RECIPE—SERVES 15

1 fifth (750 ml) Belvedere Citrus (lemon) vodka

12 oz (360 ml) Cointreau

3 pints (1.5 liter) fresh-pressed watermelon juice

2 pints (1 liter) homemade lemonade

For a fun party presentation, cut the top off a watermelon (approx. 4 inches down). Carefully scoop all the meat out of the watermelon (you can use it to make juice) while leaving the body intact. Mix up the batch in a large pitcher, refrigerate it to chill, then pour it into your watermelon punch bowl when you're ready to serve. To stabilize your watermelon bowl, cut just enough from its base to provide a flat surface. Garnish with quarter-slices of lemon and blueberries; serve in ice-filled goblets.

DRINKS BY STYLE

RESOURCES

FRIENDS AND COLLEAGUES' INTERESTING WEBSITES

Alconomics
Bar consultancy and bespoke staff
training services
www.alconomics.com

Ardent Spirits
Gary and Mardee Regan's spirit
and cocktail newsletter
www.ardentspirits.com

Dr. Cocktail's Drink Database
Extensive cocktail recipe library
www.cocktaildb.com

Drink Boy
Robert Hess's cocktail site
www.drinkboy.com

King Cocktail
Dale DeGroff's website
www.kingcocktail.com

Paul Harrington's Cocktail Database
Detailed selection of cocktail recipes
www.cocktail.com

Shaken Not Stirred:
A Celebration of the Martini
Steven Visakay's guide to classic
cocktail shakers
www.martiniplace.com/book2.html

Spirit Journal
F. Paul Pacult's spirits newsletter
www.spiritjournal.com

The Modern Mixologist
My website
www.themodernmixologist.com

The Museum of the American Cocktail
www.ThemuseumOfTheAmericanCocktail.com

United States Bartenders Guild
Nonprofit organization working to enhance
the prestige of the professional bartender
www.USBG.org

Webtender
A drink forum pertaining to the bar
www.webtender.com

BIBLIOGRAPHY

Albert, Bridget. *Market Fresh Mixology.* Agate Surrey. Chicago: 2008

Arthur, Stanley Clisby. *Famous New Orleans Drinks, and How to Mix'em.* Harmanson Publishers. Nouvelle, Orleans: 1937

Barr, Andrew. *Drink, A Social History of America.* Carroll & Graf Publishers Inc. New York: 1999

Bergeron, Victor. *Trader Vic's Bartender's Guide (revised 1972).* Doubleday & Company Inc. New York: 1972

Birmingham, Frederic A. *Esquire Drink Book.* Esquire Inc. New York: 1969

Blue, Anthony Dias. *The Complete Book of Mixed Drinks.* Harper Perennial. New York: 1993

Brennan, Georgeanne. *Apéritif.* Chronicle Books. San Francisco: 1997

Bullock, Tom, and Frienz, D.J. *173 Pre-Prohibition Cocktails.* Howling at the Moon Press. Jenks, OK: 2001

Calabrese, Salvatore. *Classic After- Dinner Drinks.* Sterling Publishing. New York: 1999

Calabrese, Salvatore. *Classic Cocktails.* Sino Publishing. China: 1997

Cecchini, Toby. *Cosmopolitan: A Bartender's Life.* Broadway Books. New York, NY: 2003

Cipriani, Arrigo. *Harry's Bar: The Life and Times of the Legendary Venice Landmark.* Arcade Publishing. New York: 1996

Conrad III, Barnaby. *Absinthe: History in a Bottle.* Chronicle Books. San Francisco: 1988

Conrad III, Barnaby. *The Martini.* Chronicle Books. San Francisco: 1995

Cotton, Leo. *Old Mr. Boston (31st Printing).* Wehman Brothers. Hackensack, NJ: 1965

Craddock, Harry. *The Savoy Cocktail Book.* Lowe & Brydone Ltd. London: 1930

Crockett, Albert Stevens. *Old Waldorf Bar Days.* Aventine Press. New York: 1931

Crockett, Albert Stevens. *The Old Waldorf-Astoria Bar Book.* A. S. Crockett New York: 1935

De Groff Dale. *The Craft of the Cocktail.* Clarkson Potter Publishers. New York: 2002

De Groff, Dale. *The Essential Cocktail.* Clarkson Potter Publishers. New York: 2008

De Voto, Bernard. *The Hour.* The Riverside Press. Massachusetts: 1951

Doxat, John. *The World of Drinks and Drinking.* Drake Publishers. New York: 1971

Duffy, Patrick Gavin. *The Official Mixer's Manual.* Doubleday & Company. New York: 1956

Edmunds, Lowell. *Martini, Straight Up.* Johns Hopkins University Press. Baltimore & London: 1998

Embury, David A. *The Fine Art of Mixing Drinks.* Country Life Press. Garden City, NY: 1948

Emmons, Bob. *The Book of Gins and Vodkas.* Open Court Publishing. Chicago: 2000

Field, Colin Peter. *The Cocktails of the Ritz Paris.* Simon & Schuster, New York: 2003

Foley, Raymond. *The Ultimate Cocktail Book II.* Foley Publishing. 1998

Frost, Griffith and Gauntner, John. *Sake Pure + Simple.* Stone Bridge Press. Berkeley, CA: 1999

Giglio, Anthony. *Cocktails in New York.* Rizzoli International Publications. New York: 2005

Grimes, William. *Straight Up or On the Rocks.* Simon & Schuster. New York: 1993

Hamilton, Edward. *The Complete Guide to Rum.* Triumph Books. Chicago: 1997

Harrington, Paul and Moorehead, Laura. *Cocktail.* Viking. New York: 1998.

Jackson, Michael. *Bar & Cocktail Companion.* Running Press. Philadelphia & London: 1995

Jackson, Michael. *The Pocket Bartender's Guide.* Simon and Schuster. New York: 1979

Kelly, Bill. *The Roving Bartender.* Oxford Press. Hollywood, CA: 1946

Lanza, Joseph. *The Cocktail.* St. Martin's Press. New York: 1995

MacElhone, Harry. *Harry's ABC's of Mixing Cocktails.* Souvenir Press. London: 1996

Mautone, Nick. *Raising the Bar.* Artisan. New York: 2004

Miller, Anistatia R., Brown, Jared M., and Gatterdam, Don. *Shaken Not Stirred.* Harper Perennial. New York: 1997

Miller, Anistatia R., and Brown, Jared M. *Champagne Cocktails* . Regan Books. New York: 1999

Miller, Anistatia R., and Brown, Jared M., editors *Mixologist: The Journal of the American Cocktail.* Mixellany. New York: 2005

Pacult, F. Paul. *Kindred Spirits.* Hyperion. New York: 1997

Knowles, Frederick Lawrence. *The Cocktail Book.* L.C. Page, & Co. Boston: 1903.

Reed, Ben. *The Art of the Cocktail.* Ryland, Peters & Small. London and New York: 2004

Regan, Gary and Regan, Mardee Haidin. *New Classic Cocktails.* Macmillan. New York: 1997

Regan, Gary and Regan, Mardee Haidin. *The Book of Bourbon.* Houghton Mifflin. Boston: 1995

Regan, Gary and Regan, Mardee Haidin. *The Martini Companion.* Running Press. Philadelphia: 1997

Regan, Gary. *The Joy of Mixology.* Clarkson Potter. New York, NY: 2003

Said, Oliver and Mellgren, James. *The Bar.* Ten Speed Press. Berkeley, CA: 2005

Schenley Products Co. *The Original Merry Mixer.* Schenley Products Co. New York: 1936

Schumann, Charles. *American Bar.* Abbeville Press Publishers. Paris & London: 1995

Siegelman, Steve. *Trader Vic's Tiki Party, Cocktails & Food to Share with Friends.* Ten Speed Press. Berkeley, CA: 2005

Thomas, Professor Jerry. *Jerry Thomas's The Bar-tenders Guide, or How to Mix All Kinds of Plain and Fancy Drinks.* Wehman Bros. New York: 1887

Thompson, Jennifer Trainer. *The Great Tiki Drink Book.* Ten Speed Press. Berkeley: 2002

Visakay, Stephen. *Vintage Bar Ware.* Collector Books. Paducah, KY: 1997

Waggoner, Susan and Markel, Robert. *Vintage Cocktails.* Smithmark Publishers. New York: 1999

Whitfield, W.C. *Here's How Mixed Drinks.* Three Mountaineers. Asheville, NC: 1941

Wondrich, David. *Imbibe!.* Perigee. New York: 2007

ACKNOWLEDGMENTS

How to begin to say thank you, to acknowledge all who have helped, either directly or indirectly, with bringing this book to life seems an impossible feat. Here's our go...

First and above all, a thousand "thank yous" to Helen for her guiding influence and a lifetime of inspiration, and to Neva for all of her smiles, support, and her adorable appreciation for a well-made Bellini. And of course to the rest of our oh-so-patient families—we recognize and appreciate each one for their inspiration, encouragement, and above all for "playing along" with our endeavor over the years... Janet, Kaitlin, Sweets, Big A, and the great team at The Modern Mixologist: Andrea, Bradley, Carol, and Ellie. The Clans Faulkner, Rolfe, and Ewing, Den, Peter and John, and to Donia and Emma for being Neva's rocks.

Special thanks go also to:
... Agate Surrey for working with our dream—Doug, Eileen, Perrin, and Diana.
... Tim "I love Manchego in the morning" Turner and the entire crew at Tim Turner Studios, for your insightful artistry and breathtaking photography.
... Christopher Bloom and Betsey Berg—attorney and agent extraordinaire, respectively.
... Match, Riedel and Spiegelau glassware for sharing their collections, and Hamilton Beach for the use of their products featured in the photography.

And so many more who have left an indelible imprint:
... Angus, for responding to a strange woman's sophomoric email, recommending Embury's book, and for every bit of kindness since... Brian, Dave, and John for sharing their vast knowledge and critical eye toward the timeline... Christina for sampling so many recipes, and falling in love with the Cable Car... Dale, for

his presence, partnership, and inspiration over the years... David, for introducing the authors way back when, support from day one, and an unending well of spirit knowledge... Floyd, for his kind encouragement, insightful editorial acumen, and one or two indelible single malt experiences... Greg, for his stunning level of patience with "the project," healthy doses of good (pointed) humor, and the use of his abode for several marathon writing sessions... Jason, Joey, and Eric from Inoteca Liquori Bar, and everyone at the Brass Rail... Julio, for always clearing the honored spot at the end of the bar, contribution to all things tequila, and for working so hard on that quote... Mario—what's to be said, except it's been a beautiful life!... Marco, for sharing his impressive and very precious book collection... Marguerite, for her patience with all those LV trips, her hyper-intelligence, and so much more... So many industry luminaries, legends, professionals, and supporters: Jacques, Bridget, Peter D, Salvatore, John, Francesco, Elmer, Steve O., Bob M., EBP partners and crew... and all others who have inspired, or just made a great cocktail.

INDEX